RED ON RED

RED ON RED

RED HOLZMAN AND
HARVEY FROMMER

BANTAM BOOKS
NEW YORK · TORONTO · LONDON · SYDNEY · AUCKLAND

RED ON RED

A Bantam Book / December 1987

Every effort has been made to contact copyright proprietors of photos not owned by Red Holzman. We regret any inadvertent omission of credit lines and would be pleased to include such lines in any future edition, where appropriate, if the omission is brought to our attention.

Book Design by Jaye Zimet

Library of Congress Cataloging-in-Publication Data

Holzman, Red.
  Red on Red.

  Includes index.
  1. Holzman, Red. 2. Basketball—United States—Coaches
—Biography. I. Frommer, Harvey. II. Title.
GV884.H65A3 1987   796.32′3′0924 [B]   87-47582
ISBN 0-553-05225-X

Published simultaneously in the United States and Canada

Bantam Books are published by Bantam Books, Inc. Its trademark, consisting of the words "Bantam Books" and the portrayal of a rooster, is Registered in U.S. Patent and Trademark Office and in other countries. Marca Registrada. Bantam Books, Inc., 666 Fifth Avenue, New York, New York 10103.

For Selma, Gail, and the fans.
And Sophie and Abraham, my parents,
who made it all possible.

ACKNOWLEDGMENTS

Various people were of great assistance in sharing their time and memories: Selma Holzman, Gail Holzman, Leonard Lewin, Gwynne Bloomfield, Butch Beard, Norman Blass, Vince Boryla, Red Phillips, Dustin Hoffman, John Hewig, Ceil and Harry Kolber, Bernie Sarachek, Eddie Donovan, Phoebe Lewin, Randy Whelan, Arnoldo Hernandez, Danny Whelan, Phil Jackson, Sonny Werblin, Ira Berkow, Lester Harrison, Nat Holman, Frank Blauschild, Harthorne Wingo, Phil Fox, Willie Vicens, Pachen Vicens, Bob and Adam Wallach, Cal Ramsey, Dick Isaacs, Cotton Fitzsimmons, and Ben Kerner, Red Rubel, Howie Hirschman, Eddie Donovan, Ned Irish, Jules Holzman, Larry Baxter, Roz Puretz, Carl Martin, John Cirillo, Al DeSibio, and John Condon. A large debt is owed George Kalinsky, an especially talented photographer.

Special thanks to Fuzzy Levane, who got me started and kept me going, and Bill Bradley for the nice things he said about me in the introduction.

Agent Artie Pine came up with the concept, and Lou Wolfe, former President of Bantam, successfully twisted my arm to do it, then introduced me to all the Hall of Fame talent at Bantam Books. Peter Guzzardi, our editor at Bantam, skillfully coached the manuscript through to fruition. Thanks also to Alison Acker, his capable and dedicated assistant. And Myrna Frommer was of invaluable help in reading and editing.

My biggest thank-you goes to Harvey Frommer, a talented and creative writer. I'm glad I made him my Number One draft choice.

R.H.

A leader is best
when people barely know he exists.
Not so good
when people obey and acclaim him.
Worse when they despise him.
But of a good leader
who talks little
when this work is done
his aim fulfilled
they will say:
"We did it ourselves."

Lao-tse (c. 565 B.C.)
on leadership

INTRODUCTION by Senator Bill Bradley

I played in the National Basketball Association for a decade with the New York Knickerbockers, and throughout virtually all that time I had just one coach—Red Holzman. However, Red became more than a coach for me; he became a trusted friend.

In Red's first year as coach we lost often, and during one twenty-five-day stretch, we played eight games and had twenty-one two-hour practices. Everyone learned quickly that under Red's rugged work ethic, life was more pleasant if we won.

Red Holzman never begged players to do good deeds, nor did he set up elaborate codes of conduct. He expected everyone to act as a responsible adult and he treated players accordingly. To rookies and substitutes he said, "If you miss a practice, it's up to you to find a place to work out on your own. Just make sure when you're called on to play you're in shape." To veterans he said, "No one drinks in the main bar of the hotel where the team stays. That one belongs to me."

His sense of humor was always at work, and it was a big asset that helped him handle the different personalities on the Knicks and the pressures of the game.

The real genius of Red Holzman was in his handling of players. A comment on a plane or in an airport might relate tangentially to a previous game, but it was always delivered low-key. "Seeing the ball" on defense and "hitting the open man" on offense were Red's constant exhortations. Some of us on the Knicks heard those words in our sleep, words that became our team's trademark.

Whether we won or lost, Red Holzman was unflappable. Shaped by all his years as a player, scout, coach, general manager, he knew that whatever happened, the next day brought another game, the next season brought a new beginning. His calm and controlled outlook influenced all our efforts.

Although pro basketball often showcases individual performers, Red's view of the game was that it was a democratic effort. The parts of the team for him were never as important as the sum of the parts. One of his greatest contributions as a coach was that he revived respect for team play, and in particular, team defense. He was relentless in his pursuit of that ideal and had the unusual ability of getting his players to willingly see it his way.

Many do not understand the press and public relations job that an NBA coach has to master. Holzman had seen six Knick coaches fired while he was the chief scout. Each victim had assisted his own demise with careless remarks in unguarded moments. Red never said anything negative about anybody to the press; if possible, he said nothing.

His low-keyed approach exasperated some sportswriters, but it enabled Red to master probably the trickiest aspect of being a Knick coach. Ernest Hemingway might have had someone like Red Holzman in mind when he defined courage as "grace under pressure."

Other books by former coaches and athletes have been hard-hitting, sensational, geared to controversy. Red Holzman's book is none of these things. Like the man whose story it tells, it is self-effacing, honest, and humorous.

Red Holzman was the right man in the right place at the right time as the coach of the New York Knicks—and I was happy to be a part of it all.

Now Red has been given the highest recognition accorded by his profession—induction into the Basketball Hall of Fame. It is a well-deserved honor, and it pleases me to know that his record will now be a permanent part of the sport we both loved so much.

RED ON RED

BOOK ONE

CHAPTER 1

The old Madison Square Garden arena, between Forty-ninth and Fiftieth Streets and between Eighth and Ninth Avenues in the heart of Manhattan, was the scene of some of the greatest action in hockey, boxing, and basketball. Being there, you couldn't help but feel its grand tradition. There was a nice holiday mood at the Garden on December 27, 1967. I was there in the press mezzanine overhang, watching a matinee game between the New York Knickerbockers and the Philadelphia Warriors. It was one of the best seats in the house. Nobody knew who I was, and I was enjoying my privacy.

I didn't know it at the time, but one weekend earlier, at a New York Giants football game, a conversation had taken place that would end my privacy and change my life. My friend Dick Isaacs and Ned Irish, the president of the New York Knickerbockers, were having the latest in a series of discussions.

"Dick," Irish said, "we're frustrated with the team. There's a lot of talent there, but they just can't seem to get it together. I'm seriously thinking of making a coaching change again. Tom Gola is the guy I have in mind to replace Dick McGuire."

"If suggestions are in order, Ned, I've got one," Dick Isaacs said. "You have a guy who's already part of the Knick family who would make a tremendous coach—Red Holzman."

"Red Holzman? Never considered him. But it's an idea. He's done a fine job as assistant coach and chief scout."

"Well, give it some thought. In my opinion, Red knows more about basketball than anyone in the game."

That December 27 the Knicks lost their fourth straight game blowing a 21-point lead. Their record dropped to 15 and 22. During the fourth quarter Knick general manager Eddie Donovan came over and told me that Ned Irish wanted to see me.

I had no idea what Irish had on his mind, but I found out pretty quick.

"The team will be making a coaching change," Irish said bluntly. "We want you to take over until the end of the season. You're going to be the new head coach."

"What did I do to deserve this?" I said, not really believing Irish was serious. When he assured me that he was, I tried to wiggle out of all the headaches and pressures that I knew came with the head coaching job.

Irish was not smiling. I could see that he had his mind made up.

"I guess I don't have much of a choice in this, right, Mr. Irish?"

"Right, Red." Irish sat up straight in his chair behind his big desk. "You don't have much of a choice. You work for the organization and we need you to take over as coach. Now."

Irish looked like he was in a rush to wrap things up. He was twiddling with a yellow pencil.

"I want to make one thing clear, Mr. Irish."

"What's that, Red?"

"I'm taking the job, but I'm taking it on an interim basis."

"That's understood."

"When the season ends I return to doing what I was doing."

"We have no problem with that," Irish said. "You'll even get a raise. You're helping us out in a pinch. And we appreciate it." Irish came out from behind the desk. We shook hands. "Good luck, Red. I know you'll do a creditable job."

I had mixed feelings at that moment. I was forty-seven years old then, and happy and satisfied with what I had been doing. There had been coaching offers from other NBA teams during the years, but I had turned them down out of loyalty to the Knicks. Also, I didn't want to leave New York City. Coaches had come and gone with the Knicks, but I had never been considered for the job. Even though I felt I had good credentials for the job, I was just as happy not to be considered. In baseball when a manager is fired everyone around him goes. It's the same way in basketball. But my job as a scout for the organization had allowed me to survive all the changes. Now I'd be right on the firing line.

After Irish and I finished our talk, I caught up with my wife, Selma, who was waiting for me outside the press box.

"The Knicks have a brand-new coach," I told her.

"Who?"

"Me."

"Oh, my God!" Selma was shocked.

We both knew we were in for a big change. As a scout I had been obscure, out of the limelight. There was never much pressure on me and Selma, and we both liked it that way. Now I was going to be coach of the New York Knickerbockers in the media capital of the world. Things in our lives would never be quite the same again. Still, I knew she was pleased that I had been asked to take over. And somewhere, deep inside, I was too.

After I spoke to Selma, Irish wasted no time bringing me into the Knickerbocker locker room. "Fellows, we have decided to make a coaching change," he announced. "You all know Red Holzman. He's now your new head coach. Dick McGuire will take over Red's old job as chief scout."

Some of the players wished me well. Others, I could tell, felt sorry for Dick. I told them there would be a meeting the next morning at ten. Then I gave some interviews to the press. By the time I arrived home that night in Cedarhurst, Long Island, it was pretty late.

I poured myself a Dewar's White Label, sat down in my favorite chair, and thought about life's strange twists. I thought about all the times I was at Madison Square Garden as a fan, a player, a coach, a scout. I thought about how the NBA had been totally transformed in my twenty-two years in pro ball, about the old owners who had sat on the bench and coached their teams, and the new corporate owners who now sat in their private boxes. I thought of how the league had changed with the arrival of bigger, faster, stronger, more talented players.

I had always been a movie fan. My favorite film is the life story of George M. Cohan—*Yankee Doodle Dandy* with James Cagney. It begins with a flashback. The screen grows hazy. Cagney goes back in time. As I sat in my chair my mind flashed back. I thought back over the years of my life that had brought me to this crossroads point in time. . . .

I was born on the Lower East Side of Manhattan on August 10, 1920, and moved to Brooklyn with my family when I was four years old. It was as though we had moved to the country. The neighborhood was mostly Italians and Jews. We lived in the Ocean Hill–Brownsville section on the third floor of a tenement at 2110 Atlantic Avenue off Saratoga Avenue. In those days you could come home at two or three in the morning and still feel safe.

My mother, Sophie, and my father, Abraham, came from the old country. My mother came from Romania, and my father was from a little place on the Russian border. My brother, Julie, and my sister, Minnie, both older than I, lived with us, along with my uncle Leon and his daughter Celia. Minnie and Celia were only a few months apart in age and slept in the same room and went out together. They were like close sisters, and my mother encouraged that.

I was out in the streets all the time, playing ball, while my brother, Julie, was dutifully working. My playing ball didn't go over too big with my parents. Uncle Leon was something of a sports fan, but my father had no interest in games except for soccer. He worked very hard just to keep things going.

My mother, the backbone of the family, was a terrific cook and made every meal taste as if you were eating it for the first time in your life. My father was a tailor, and although he was not a big earner, we always ate well. My mother found a way, somehow, and she could feed forty people on nothing. Romanians are great cooks and wine drinkers and love to have a good time. I picked up my taste for food with character and my love of life from my mother.

The extended family unit was our main source of entertainment. Friends were always dropping by, asking, "What time do we eat?"

Sunday afternoons were a popular time for visiting. Loads of people would come by, have a big, satisfying meal, some wine, look for a bed or their favorite nook, and take a nap. Our home looked like a dormitory on Sunday afternoons.

One of the closest friends of the family was Morris Barth, who was only about five feet tall but worth his weight in gold. Morris was an expert in *"schtelen bonkers,"* the art of placing glass cups with alcohol in them on your body. Morris would heat the cups and draw out a cold or a fever. In those days people would go to the beach with *bonkers* (cup marks) all over them, and you knew they had gone through the treatment.

My father's work was seasonal, with slack times when there wasn't much work. Then he'd be down in the dumps and worry about money. But my mother was always able to keep it all together no matter what. My father didn't need too much to make him happy—a walk, a breeze, something good to eat and drink, an occasional trip to the country. My father was a great family man, and I was very close to him and my mother.

After a couple of years of living in the tenement, we moved around the corner to a place above a butcher shop at 299 Saratoga Avenue. There was no air-conditioning, and on summer nights with the windows open in my bedroom I was able to get a hell of an education. Back then relatives often all lived together and not always in harmony. Fist fights, sexual squabbling, bickering over money, gossip—I heard it all, with the choicest of street language thrown in for good measure.

One guy named Schnitz would come home about three in the morning every Saturday night and wake up the whole neighborhood singing: "Why did I have to get married to get tied to that ball 'n chain?/My wife is a stone-hearted jailer, and she treats all the men the same."

Around the corner from where I lived was St. Clair McEllway School. I quickly became a school-yard rat there, playing soccer, football, handball, softball, baseball, and especially basketball.

My father was always concerned about me making the wrong friends.

"Pop," I excitedly described one of my new acquaintances, "this guy is cool."

In my father's mind the word *cool* must have made him think the guy was doing something he should not be doing. *"Roita,"* (that was his Yiddish word for Red) *"vere is dere kool? Luzmer him zayn."* (Translated: "Where is the cool—let me see him.") My father wanted to check him out.

Yiddish was all we spoke for many years at home and I really loved the sound of the language, with all its colorful and not quite translatable expressions. *Narishket* (foolishness) was a word my parents used to describe my ball playing.

Back then they had what they called "four foot ten" teams that were organized by the local schools in the summer. You had to be that height or less to play. To my regret I was able to play for quite a few summers.

After a while I became so good at sports that I spent all my time playing ball. My parents wanted me to study. I wanted to play ball. Some nights, in order to play at the neighborhood center I would have to throw my shoes and equipment out the back window of our apartment and then fumble around in the dark in the courtyard searching for them.

I was also a pretty good handball player in the school yards. I was a hustler and since I was small everybody thought I was a little kid and that they could easily beat me. Many times my winnings ran as high as two or three dollars a day. Since we played for a quarter a game, that was a hell of a lot of money.

A kid who came over from Italy, Nunzio, was even smaller than I, but he refused to play handball against me unless it was on his court, a place in the school yard that had a wall with an indentation. Since I knew my chances of winning weren't too good against him on his court, I played him for a nickel, never for a quarter. I lost a lot of nickels but I liked the challenge. That kid and his wall taught me the value of the home court advantage at a very early age.

The first organized sport I became interested in was soccer. My father and my uncle Leon would take me every Sunday to the Polo Grounds or Hawthorne Field in Brooklyn. Even if it was raining or bitter cold or a blizzard, we would always go. My uncle had the car— one year he even had a Nash open touring car with a running board. A highlight of that time was watching the Hakoah All Stars—a great professional soccer team from Vienna—at the Polo Grounds.

My uncle was a New York Giants fan living in Brooklyn, and although I liked the Dodgers, he converted me to rooting for the Giants. We would go to the Polo Grounds and watch Mel Ott, Carl Hubbell, and Freddy Fitzsimmons. But of all the sports, basketball was the one I always liked the best. My uncle Leon would take me to see the Brooklyn Jewels play at Arcadia Hall on Halsey Street in the Bushwick section of Brooklyn. The Jewels had been the St. John's "Wonder Five" and had all turned pro together, joining the American League.

Divided into thirds rather than halves, those games produced only about 35 or 40 points. The two-hand set shot was used almost exclusively, and the two-hand dribble was a special feature of those games. Rules specified that a player had to dribble forward or else he'd lose the ball. You were not allowed to screen a player out or you would lose the ball. You were not allowed to shoot with your back to the basket when you were inside. There was a small lane and you could stay in there all day, so you can imagine there'd be a great deal of pushing and shoving. It was a rough game.

Mac Kinsbrunner was the star of the Jewels, and he was a master dribbler who could control the ball all night. I sat in the stands and studied his every move. And for a week after that I would be Kinsbrunner as I tried out what I had seen him do on anybody I could get to play against me.

Another basketball team that I went out of my way to see was the Harlem Renaissance Five, known as the Rens. An all-black team, they played on Sunday nights in the Renaissance Casino nightclub in Harlem and used to come to Arcadia Hall to go against the Jewels.

The Rens, founded by Bob Douglas in 1922, were unlike the Harlem Globetrotters, who were more show business than basketball. For that time there was probably no better basketball team in the world than the Rens. From 1932 to 1936 they won 473 games against just 49 losses. They played one-night stands and traveled and slept in their own custom-made "$10,000 bus." Games were played on unfamiliar courts against town teams who hired the refs, and often they would be very physical. But the Rens played so many games that they knew each other's moves instinctively. They played a switching man-to-man defense to save extra steps and conserve energy and emphasized team basketball and unselfishness. Their style made a big impression on me and I filed it away for future reference.

I played as much basketball as I could at Junior High School 178 even though there was no formal basketball program there. When I graduated to Franklin K. Lane High School I played on both the handball and basketball teams.

Lane did not have a gym, and we practiced in the school yard and played all our games on the courts of our opponents. Although I did well, our team was handicapped by lack of proper facilities.

One game especially remains in my mind. Leo Merson had been a top player at Long Island University and was the basketball coach at Alexander Hamilton High School. His mind was always working. We came in for the first time to play his team, which had a great scorer, Jim White, who later went on to star for St. John's.

I had developed a reputation as a tough defensive player and Merson was worried that I would eat White up. So he switched White's uniform number for that game. I went in there and hounded the guy who was supposed to be White. I murdered him, but White murdered us. We lost the game. Every time I see Merson he kids me about that game. "Sure, you're a bigshot," I tell him. "You took advantage of a high school kid."

That incident taught me at a very early age that it doesn't pay to ever take anything for granted on a basketball court.

At the same time I played for Lane I also played for the Workmen's Circle, a fraternal organization team coached by Red Sarachek. He helped out at Lane and later became the coach at Yeshiva University. Red and the older guys on the Workmen's Circle team taught me a great deal about playing unselfish basketball.

It was during this time that I first met Selma. Her parents belonged to the Workmen's Circle, and she was a volleyball player. I was interested in her right from the start, but I didn't date her right away because I was pretty shy in those days.

When I graduated from Franklin K. Lane High School in 1938, the school had already moved into a new building in Jamaica, Queens. Little did I dream that thirty-nine years later I would return to Lane for the dedication of the William Red Holzman Gymnasium.

After graduation, in order to help out my family I worked for Local 102 pushing a hand wagon through the streets of New York City's garment center. It was backbreaking work, and rough in bad weather, but I was making $29.50 a week. That was a lot of money, especially for the first real job I had ever had.

I also had grown quite a bit. All my people were short. I was almost five foot ten then. My family had never seen anyone that size close up, and to them I seemed like a giant. My newly acquired height and the money I was making made me a little cocky.

"Pop, you can retire now," I told my father. "I'll take care of everything."

"*De k-nocker,* (you bigshot) you're going to support me?" He reached up and grabbed me around the neck. I knew he was just horsing around because he was careful not to squeeze. "I'll throw you out the window."

I pushed the handtruck weekdays and spent my evenings and weekends playing basketball for Local 102, which had the best amateur team in New York City. We played against tough competition, and my game improved even more.

I played for Local 102 for about a year. Then Phil Fox, a local ref who later became an NBA referee, helped me get a basketball scholarship to the University of Baltimore. I would have loved to have attended college in New York City, but I was willing to give Baltimore a try since they were willing to give me a try.

Baltimore was building a team under coach Bucky Miller and a good bunch of players came in there as freshmen. We played against name teams like Stanford, Tulane, LIU, and we beat a lot of them. But all the while I kept hoping I'd get back to New York City. The food in Baltimore was foreign—not like the soul food that my mother made. There wasn't much of it either, and I was always hungry. I missed my folks. I missed Selma. And after six months I transferred to the City College of New York.

I didn't have a scholarship so I brown-bagged my lunches, but with Nat Holman as my coach at City College it was a whole new world. One of the great players in his days with the "original Celtics," Nat Holman was also one of the greatest coaches of all time. When he coached me he was in his late forties, trim, a tough squash player, and a guy who believed in keeping himself in shape. His attitude as a coach was "distant nearness." Nat was friendly but only to a point. He never let the line between player and coach get blurred.

His understanding of the game was one of his strong traits, and he taught you with an eye to your playing pro ball. Nat believed very strongly in five-man movement. He called it five moving pivots. Each man met the ball as a pivot and made a play for someone else. He had good theories about team defense, and I picked up a lot of insights in that area from him. I also learned not to hold the ball. That was one of the things Nat didn't like, and he was constantly after me about it. I guess much of my feeling for ball movement came from my association with him.

Nat Holman always gave me the toughest guy to guard. Defense was hard work, but I was in great shape in those days and could run all night. I tried to make defense fun. Nat tutored me in denying the passing lanes. And I innovated the technique of playing a big guy from the front to deny him the ball. My City College team didn't lose a single game to a metropolitan area team, and I was an all-American for two seasons.

In the summer of 1942 I put on a new uniform. I enlisted in the United States Navy. My life and that of millions of others was affected by World War II. My parents weren't too happy that I had joined up, but instead of being drafted I gave myself a choice. I had heard good things about the Navy.

I was stationed at Norfolk Naval Base and placed in the morale unit, which drilled and exercised troops and maintained recreational facilities. In our time off we also played basketball against other service and college teams. Those service teams had tremendous athletes. Norfolk's baseball team had Phil Rizzuto, Vince DiMaggio, Freddie Hutchinson, Pee Wee Reese, Hugh Casey. All our games took place before enthusiastic, packed houses and the style of play was very physical.

When I had first arrived at Norfolk, I was a seaman first class—the only sailor playing with chief petty officers. After a while I became a chief too. Our coach, Gary Bodie, was an old chief warrant officer. He knew how to motivate. "Get your ass moving," he'd yell, "or you'll be on a ship to the Pacific tomorrow." We moved our asses. Our Norfolk team was real good. One year we won 31 of the 33 games we played.

Rizzuto always used his spare time to polish his baseball skills, especially his pivoting at shortstop to make the double play. I would toss the ball to him and he'd complain that I threw a heavy ball.

We were both from New York City and we had a lot in common so we became pretty friendly. I was the unofficial adviser for "Rizzuto's Ragamuffins," a baseball team that competed against the Naval Air Force Squad coached by Pee Wee Reese.

Whenever I was able to get a weekend pass I would drive back to New York City. One weekend I was heading back along with Phil Rizzuto and stopped off to phone Selma. It was then that I learned we were getting married.

"My parents have picked out a fancy restaurant, Red," she said. "The wedding is set for this weekend."

It was a bit of a surprise, and we sure had to make our plans in a hurry. Since I was in the service, they gave us a break on the blood test, so we didn't have to wait the usual three days for the results. As for the wedding, Selma's parents handled that. We were married at a place called Garfein's on the Lower East Side, one of those big banquet halls with a small temple adjoining. Anyone who had a telephone got invited, and in all we managed to round up about eighty friends and relatives for the festivities. I was married in my Navy uniform, but other than that I really can't remember a damn thing about the wedding itself except that I got what I wanted: Selma. Marrying Selma was the best thing I ever did in my life.

As a married man I was able to live in an apartment with Selma off base for nearly three years. We had a spare bedroom and guys we were friends with would sometimes stay over, shoot the breeze, and get a home-cooked meal.

The first time we had Phil Rizzuto over for dinner was unforgettable. Selma was excited that a baseball celebrity would be our guest. So she went all out planning a menu that she thought would appeal to him.

Phil arrived. We had drinks. We settled down at the table. Selma served her appetizer. Tomato juice. "The stuff is thirst-quenching," said Selma. "It's a good way to start a meal, Phil."

"You bet." Rizzuto was polite. He gulped down the juice and wiped his lips with a napkin. That was his way of indicating he was ready for the next dish.

It was a Spanish omelette stuffed with tomatoes. Phil ate it up and then went to the napkin again. Selma walked back into the kitchen and brought out her next course. Tomato soup.

Phil picked. Phil ate. Phil wiped his lips with the napkin, which was getting redder and redder.

"How do you like the food?" Selma asked.

"Fine, just fine." Phil smiled. "Only I hope you don't have tomato pie for dessert."

Most of my last year in the Navy was spent at Treasure Island and Shoemaker, California, about forty-five minutes from San Francisco. Selma and I lived on base and the California style of life was very comfortable. Aside from the beautiful location, the security of making the Navy a career was tempting, but ever since I had been a little kid I'd had the dream of becoming a professional basketball player, and I did not want to give that up. Navy basketball helped by giving me the experience of going against top athletes from all over the country, boosting my confidence, and convincing me that I could be a pro player.

With the war finally ending, I made my decision to go back to civilian life. I used some of those last few months in the Navy to keep in shape in a big field house that had basketball courts. Selma and I were the only ones there and we felt like a couple of kids let loose to play in a big gym as we ran together up and down the court. I played against Selma one on one and once in a while I beat her, but then again I had a height advantage.

CHAPTER 2

When World War II ended I was discharged from the Navy. I was twenty-five years old, and all I really knew anything about was playing basketball. I found a way to make some money and have fun at the same time by becoming a free-lance pro, playing on a pay-per-game basis for local town teams and the New York Gothams in the American League.

Back in my college days I had made friends with Fuzzy Levane. He was a big star on St. John's, and I had a good reputation playing for CCNY. We worked together for a couple of summers in the Adirondacks at Scaroon Manor, where they made the movie *Marjorie Morningstar* (not then, later on). Fuzzy was a waiter and I was a busboy. We wore white jackets on the job, and at the end of the day you could tell every meal Fuzzy had served just by looking at his jacket. Strawberries for breakfast, steak for lunch, vegetable soup for dinner.

Fuzzy had spent the war years in the Coast Guard and afterward joined the Rochester Royals in the National Basketball League. The team's owner, Les Harrison, thinking Fuzzy Levane was Jewish, was sure he would appeal to the team's many Jewish fans. But Fuzzy was (and is) Italian. So Harrison told Fuzzy: "Get me a Jewish player. I don't care if he can play or not. Just make sure he's Jewish."

For the first few games all I was making good at was filling out my uniform, sitting on the bench. Then one night we were getting blown out in a game against Sheboygan and Les had committed everyone to the massacre except me.

"Time for Red, Les?" Fuzzy called out.

For a moment all Les did was give Fuzz a "what-are-you-busting-my-chops-for?" stare.

"C'mon, Les." Fuzzy was determined. "Why don't you put Red in there? He's not just Jewish. He's also a pretty good ballplayer."

I went in and played a hell of a game and we wound up beating Sheboygan.

Back in those days teams had what they called "sticks," players hired for ethnic or local appeal who spent the games mainly sitting on the bench. I always look back on that game as the one that saved me from a budding career as a "Jewish stick."

One of the more interesting guys on our Rochester team was Chuck Connors, who had come out of Seton Hall University and then the American League. He was not a star, but he was tall for those days, about six eight, and could really run the floor. Chuck was a character. In the American League he was known for performing handstands across the basketball court. Chuck's captive audience at Rochester was his fellow players.

He would recite "Casey at the Bat," and I don't mean just once or twice.

Guys complained that they didn't want to hear it anymore. And Chuck would tell them to shut up, claiming that he was destined to become a great actor. I don't know if he ever became a great actor, but he certainly did a lot of stuff in Hollywood—and is still going strong.

Al Cervi was probably the first real great pro basketball player who never went to college, although college was the traditional route to the pros even then—like the minor leagues in baseball. His nickname on the Royals was "the Digger," and he lived up to it. Al was a little sensitive that he hadn't gone to college, and whenever he came up against a guy who had been A college, All-American Al worked extra hard to outplay him. Cervi went on to become one of the greatest pro guards I ever saw; he also had a fine coaching career. When he began with the pros he was just a kid off the sandlots. Today that route to the pros doesn't exist anymore.

Fuzzy Levane was an underrated player handicapped by lack of stamina and some injuries during his pro career. One time he broke his nose smashing into Moline's Don Otten, who outweighed him by about a hundred pounds. Fuzzy's nose was worked on the next day by a horse doctor in Oshkosh, and the treatment would have been fine for a horse, but it created some problems for a human being.

Bob Davies teamed with Bobby Wanzer on the Royals, creating the first famous backcourt duo in pro basketball history. Davies, a blond, good-looking, all-American type with great speed, was a guy from a suburban background who pioneered and perfected the behind-the-back dribble. Wanzer, out of a city background, was a bread-and-butter type player, steady, a guy with great instincts. Davies and Wanzer, opposites on and off the court, caught the fancy of the fans and the writers.

All the guys on my Rochester team played Eastern-style basketball. We used the back door, give and go, hitting the open man, keeping the ball moving, a lot of free-lance play. And we were real good at it, winning 24 of our 34 games. I posted the fifth best scoring average in the league that 1945–46 season and became the iron man of the Royals, playing almost every minute of every game. I won the Rookie of the Year award and was on the All-League first team.

It was a great year for me and it was also a great year for the Rochester Royals—a brand new team in the NBL. We went on to beat out Fort Wayne for the championship.

Our victory surprised a lot of people since Fort Wayne had won three straight championships. During the war years Fort Wayne's players had worked in the piston factory controlled by their owner, Fred Zollner, and that's how they got their name. A very wealthy man, Zollner was used to having his team win, and he was not too happy when things changed.

Our owner, Lester Harrison, was not a rich man, but he knew basketball and what he had to do to keep a team going. Les sold ads and tickets, and booked games. He was also one of the first owners to hire a trainer. Les was only about forty years old then, but to us he seemed ancient.

Les was kind of new at some things even though he had been around. When we first went on the road he told us, "You guys eat anything you want. The club will pay for it." We were young and energetic and we ate like pigs. We spared none of his expense. Les wanted to keep his players happy, but after that he put a five-dollar-a-day meal allowance into effect. That wasn't enough for me. I was considered one of the best eaters for a small man in the NBL. I would eat lightly before a game but afterward . . . a couple of beers, shrimp cocktail, a big steak, salad. I never skimped on food.

As our Rochester team caught on, we played a lot of exhibition games and drew like crazy. Exhibition games weren't counted in the standings, of course, but in those days we had to do it to make a few bucks to survive. That first year we must have played a hundred exhibition games in addition to 34 league games. We were out almost every night of the week playing basketball.

"C'mon," Les would say, "we'll go down to Pittston and play a game and have some fun. I'll buy some apples and corned beef sandwiches for you on the way."

We would pile into big, roomy cars and eat the apples and corned beef sandwiches and tell each other funny stories. We played town teams, club teams, everybody. On the way home from games we'd settle back in the car and listen to the mystery programs on the radio. Les usually had the best insights and was able to guess before any of us who the murderer was.

Jack Harrison was Les's younger brother. A lawyer, Jack did all the legal work for the team. When we played those exhibition games, either Jack or Les would carry around a brown paper bag that looked like their lunch. Actually, it was a bag for the guaranteed gate receipts—five hundred dollars in singles, maybe a hundred dollars in coins.

Our home games were a treat, especially since we didn't lose too many. Anyone who was anyone came to our games. It was go to the game and dinner afterward—a Rochester Saturday night ritual, a dress-up night. Men wore good suits and women put on their best dresses. Families came to the game and young marrieds, and political types came to be seen.

The Edgerton Park Arena was like a big barn with just one row of seats behind each basket. The benches where the players sat were very low so fans could look over them and see the game. Lots of guys complained that the benches were back-breakers. I didn't sit too much in those years so the bench never bothered me.

Behind each basket was a swinging door, and if a player drove too violently, he could go through the swinging door and out onto the street and usually wind up in a snowbank. (There was always a lot of snow in Rochester.) The swinging doors behind the opposing basket opened onto a narrow entrance aisle. There were times when a fan would come late to the game and be carrying a hot dog and a soda down that aisle. A player would drive for a lay-up and go through the sliding doors. The fan, the player, the hot dog, and the soda would all scatter in different directions.

Games on the road were always filled with some kind of adventure. Today life in pro basketball involves a lot of moving about, but it's in comfortable surroundings. There's even a rule that all NBA players must fly first class. Back then travel conditions were rugged.

After some Saturday night games in Rochester we'd catch a sleeper to Waterloo, Indiana, and arrive about 5:30 on a Sunday morning. We'd get off the train into the cold pitch-black air and walk alongside the railroad tracks toward the town. Like vagabonds, guys would be half asleep, holding their pants, their bags, their shoes.

There was always this man waiting for us with his wife. They owned a coffee shop called the Green Parrot Cafe. We'd stagger in and it was like finding a warm oasis. I can still remember the taste of those breakfasts—the farm-fresh eggs, the strong hot coffee, the sizzling bacon, the sweet syrup on the griddle cakes. We'd have our fill and then get into cabs and take the half-hour ride into Fort Wayne, check into the hotel, and sleep until game time.

Games against the Pistons were played in the North Side High School gym, where a four-foot wall surrounded the court like a moat. Some called that court the "bucket of blood" because of the rabid fans who showered it with all kinds of crap from the stands.

Fort Wayne was a tough place for a visiting team, but Oshkosh, Wisconsin, was no bargain either. There the local police chief always reffed the games, and he wasn't afraid to blow the whistle.

Professional basketball's color line was broken in 1946–47 when

Dolly King joined the Rochester Royals. "If he can play he can play," Les Harrison told reporters when he signed Dolly and Pop Gates, whom he sold to Buffalo.

Dolly King had starred in football, baseball, and basketball at Long Island University. Fuzzy and I roomed with Dolly that year and felt kind of protective toward him.

On the road bigots shouted racial slurs at Dolly. In Indianapolis at the Claypool Hotel the whole team wound up eating in the utility room of the kitchen when service was refused to Dolly in the restaurant. After that Fuzzy and I made up our minds to eat in the hotel room with Dolly.

There really weren't that many problems for Dolly—there shouldn't have been any. However, he was always aware that there could be an incident, a racial explosion. Dolly avoided talking much about racial issues and just went about his business of playing basketball.

About six foot five and very powerfully built, Dolly would always indulge in a small glass of sherry with a raw egg in it before he started on his breakfast. "This drink builds up your muscles," he said. "You guys should try it." Fuzzy and I tried it once—once was enough for us to spend a morning together throwing up.

Fuzzy and I did a lot of things together in those days just after World War II. We visited an Army hospital in Bath, New York, about thirty miles from Rochester. Quite a few of the guys there were really racked up and some were basket cases. It was sad being there, but we figured we'd try to cheer them up a bit.

We walked around from guy to guy, introducing ourselves and making small talk. Fuzzy stuttered a lot then and it took him a while to introduce himself.

"Hi, I'm F-F-F-F-F-Fuzzy L-L-L-L-L-L-Levane." I heard him struggle to get the words out to one patient after another. "N-n-n-nice to m-m-m-meet you."

We were in the hospital for about an hour, going through the wards and shooting the breeze. "Hi, I'm Tom Brown." It was Fuzzy's voice but his introduction had changed.

"Hey, Fuzz," I pulled him aside. "What kind of games are you playing? Who the hell is Tom Brown?"

"Nobody, Red, but F-F-F-F-Fuzzy L-L-L-L-Levane is kind of

tough for me to say over and over again. Tom Brown is nice and short."

Selma also wound up with a little difficulty with her last name. She would come to all the Rochester home games and sit in the stands, watch the action, and mingle with the fans.

One night I had a particularly good game and was swarmed over by the fans and some of the newspaper guys. Selma was at my side and she got some of the spillover attention.

A guy asked her for her autograph. "Are you sure you want my autograph?" Selma asked the guy. It was the first time in her life that anyone had ever made that request.

"Oh, yes, please!" The guy was an excitable type.

Selma signed. The guy looked at her John Hancock.

The guy sighed. "Aren't you Red Holzman's wife?"

"I am."

"But the name you signed is Selma Puretz."

Selma had gotten so overcome by the moment that she wound up signing her maiden name.

"That's okay, buddy," I cut in, taking Selma off the hook. "That's her pen name." The guy didn't know a pen name from a pencil name, but he thought he was getting a bargain so he walked away satisfied.

"Selma," I kidded, "if you want to be a star, you've got to go under your real name—no aliases. We Holzmans need all the publicity we can get."

After playing in every Royal game in the 1947–48 season I was named to the National Basketball League All-Star team for the third year in a row. That year my Rochester team lost to the Minneapolis Lakers in the NBL championship series. It was also George Mikan's first season on the Lakers, and I knew he would give me and the others who played against him fits in the years ahead.

At six ten, and a burly 255 pounds including his glasses, Mikan was the first dominant force in pro basketball. He was Superman on the basketball court. Able to set screens, pass the ball, play defense, shoot a hell of a hook, even dribble pretty well when he had to, Mikan was the complete player. And he was helped a lot on the Lakers by Jim Pollard, a six five passing forward out of Stanford.

A guy on the Lakers who wasn't much of a scorer, Tony Jaros, used to murder us by getting last-second baskets. And he'd love to rub it in.

"Hey, Red," Tony would tease after a game. "George Mikan and I got thirty-two tonight." Jaros had a good head for arithmetic—his two points and Mikan's 30 gave them 32.

Points by Mikan and Pollard in game four of the NBL finals gave the championship to the Lakers. They combined for 46 points, just 19 less than our entire team.

In an attempt to counter Mikan's talent, our owner, Les Harrison, spent $25,000 to acquire Arnie Risen from Indianapolis in 1947. That was a lot of money back then, but big guys with talent were tough to come by. Arnie was a fine player with a lot of heart but was always overmatched against Mikan, who had too much height and weight going for him.

Once Les even brought in a seven foot eight high school player named Max Palmer as a possible counter to Mikan. We were scheduled to play Minneapolis, and the kid sat near our bench just before the game. Mikan came over and the kid stood up and looked down at George.

"There ought to be a law against these big jerks," Mikan said. "They should bar them from the game."

"Yeah, George"—I raised myself to my full five foot ten—"and they should start with you."

Max Palmer was not the answer to our problems. The kid could barely walk and we had to hand him the ball before he could put it into the basket. Max Palmer stayed with us for a couple of days, and they say he drank every drop of whiskey he could get his hands on. Then he went home, but while he was around he sure was something to look up to.

George Mikan would have been something to look up to in any era. He was a mean, tough guy, but he also had a sense of humor. Once I had the misfortune of going against him in a foul line jump ball situation. George tapped the ball into the basket from the foul line.

"That's the way to do it, you big schmuck," I yelled in frustration.

George smiled. His knowledge of Yiddish was nil. So I continued to compliment him throughout the game.

A few weeks later we played the Lakers again. Mikan came

charging at me as if he were going to strangle me. "I found out what that word *schmuck* means, Red. You're gonna get it from me now!"

I got the hell out of his way. Fortunately, George was only kidding around. He could have killed me without breaking a sweat if he wanted to.

Rochester, Minneapolis, Fort Wayne, and Indianapolis all left the NBL in 1948–49 and joined the two-year-old Basketball Association of America. Getting the Lakers and Royals gave the BAA the two best pro teams around as well as basketball's drawing card—George Mikan. Home teams kept gate receipts in the BAA, giving them a nice payday with Mikan as an attraction.

Things were tough in the early years for the BAA, a league that was an offshoot of an association of hockey arena owners. The BAA had to survive a lot of growing pains, foul-ups, and primitive conditions.

The New York Knickerbockers, one of the original BAA teams under Ned Irish who had pioneered college basketball doubleheaders at Madison Square Garden, made an effort to go first class. They were one of the first teams to charter a plane, *Father Knickerbocker*. Knick players told stories about how slow that plane was. It took almost two hours to go from Trenton, New Jersey to New York City, and that was with a strong tail wind blowing. Once they left the plane door open for a couple of hours as it stood on the runway in Boston. The plane's steep aisle froze up and the pilot and the players rolled and slid down on their hands and knees to get to their seats.

Maurice Podoloff, BAA commissioner, was five feet tall and five feet wide, a brilliant man who was great at details. His family built the New Haven Arena and owned the American Hockey League franchise. Once there was a BAA game there and they forgot to supply basketballs. A guy was sent out to the local sporting goods store and the game was held up until he returned with some balls.

The Royals and the Lakers, being the new kids on the block in the BAA, were both placed in the Western Division, which made it impossible for them to meet for the championship since the divisional winner moved on to the finals. It wasn't the fairest arrangement, and Les Harrison wasn't too happy about it, but he realized that the new league was the coming thing and he wanted to be part of it.

Another coming thing was a shot pioneered in the pros by "Jumping Joe" Fulks of Philadelphia. At six five and 190 pounds, Fulks had a great touch and an assortment of spinning one-handers and running shots with either hand. However, his Sunday punch was his jump shot, an unstoppable tactic for that time. Fulks shocked everybody in the league on February 10, 1949, when he poured in a record 63 points against Indianapolis. Many teams back then had never scored that many points in an entire game. The jump shot juiced up the game, created much more offense, placed more pressure on the defense. It was clear that the shot would change the whole nature of scoring.

Perhaps the most historic moment in the history of pro basketball took place in 1949–50. The Basketball Association of America expanded to seventeen teams, 200 players, and three divisions. It also changed its name, and that's when the National Basketball Association was born.

Former NBL teams were placed in the Western Division: Anderson, Tri-Cities (Moline and Rock Island, Illinois, and Davenport, Iowa), Sheboygan, Waterloo, and Denver. One of the most unusual events in pro sports also took place when a brand new team, the Indianapolis Olympians, joined the NBA. The bulk of the talent on Indianapolis was the stars of the Kentucky University club that had competed in the 1948 Olympics. Cliff Barker, a rookie, coached the Olympians. Ralph Beard, a great guard, was a vice-president. Another star, "Wah Wah" Jones, was the secretary, and Joe Holland was a player and the treasurer. The club president was "Babe" Kimbrough, a Lexington, Kentucky sports editor, who had graduated with the team. The best Olympian of all was Alex Groza. At six seven, fast and mobile, he averaged 23.4 points a game—second only to Mikan. With all that talent, Indianapolis easily finished first in the Western Division. It was as if the Georgetown team of 1984, with Pat Ewing, had joined the NBA as a franchise.

Syracuse came in from the NBL and was put in the Eastern Division. They played at the State Fair Coliseum, a tough place for a visiting team. Sometimes fans pulled on the guide wires to the backboard when visiting teams were shooting, and refs got so much flack that they ran off the court without their police escort when games ended just to get the hell out of there in one piece. Maybe that's why Syracuse won all but one of its 31 home games that year.

My Rochester team outdid them, winning all but one of our 34 home games for a .971 percentage, the best in NBA history for a long time.

Les Harrison came into our dressing room after we lost that one game and threw chairs and cursed like a madman.

"You slobs," he shouted, "why the hell did you have to screw up our perfect record? You bums are stealing your own money."

That was his style, and I picked up a little piece of that for future reference. Complacency was a trap he never let our team to fall into.

Les picked his spots when he yelled, knew who to yell at, who to leave alone, who to stroke, who to agitate. He was the driving force that kept us playing as a team, and he was a big believer in team basketball—all for one and one for all. I tucked that knowledge away for future reference too.

Another one of his tricks of the trade was using guys in special roles. Some of the Rochester guys were designated scorers—Bobby Davies and Bobby Wanzer could hit the deep outside shots or drive if they had to; Arnie Risen could score or pass off from the pivot with equal skill; others were on the team to rebound—Arnie Johnson and Jack Coleman could bang with the best of them; still others were defensive specialists. All of us could pass the ball, move without the ball, set each other up, play unselfishly.

From 1949 to 1954 we won just one less regular season game than the Minneapolis Lakers. We were a great basketball team. Minneapolis was another great basketball team. Unfortunately for us, they had George Mikan, our old nemesis, who led them to their second straight championship in 1949–50.

Spring took its time coming to Rochester that year. It seemed there was more snow than ever. Winters there lasted until May. Being beach people, Selma and I really looked forward to the summers, when we would return to New York City. We'd rent a place in the Rockaways or Long Beach and get the chill of the Rochester winters out of our bones.

By the summer of 1950 we were a family of three. My daughter, Gail, was a little toddler then. The three of us and my in-laws rented a four-family house in Long Beach with some longtime friends. The atmosphere reminded me of my growing-up years in Brooklyn. A communal clothesline criss-crossed the back of the house. Automatic dryers weren't around much in those days, so the clothesline got a real workout—especially since we were in a resort area.

Selma remembers that time as the summer of the jockstrap mystery. She got her first clue when we were packing up in late August to return to Rochester. It was then she discovered I had a box loaded with jockstraps, sizes small, medium, and large. "Red," she said, "where'd you get all these jocks from?"

"I don't know," I answered, "I brought only a couple with me."

Selma was determined to solve the jockstrap mystery. As it turned out, Selma's mother had only girls in her family and never saw a jockstrap until she did my laundry. She didn't know what the thing was called, but she thought it was a special device used only by basketball players. Mrs. Gordon, our next door neighbor, had four athletic sons, all of whom were in and out of jocks that summer. Every time she hung one on the line, Selma's mother thought it was mine, took it in, and put it in a carton where I kept my athletic gear. Mrs. Gordon, meanwhile, was all in an uproar over the disappearance of the jockstraps. Day after day she complained to Selma's mother that someone was stealing the jockstraps. Selma's mother had no idea what jockstraps were, but she sympathized with Mrs. Gordon, who kept spending money to replace the stolen items.

Selma finally figured everything out and the jocks were returned to Mrs. Gordon's sons. Peace was restored to the neighborhood. The summer ended on a good note for everybody. Selma, Gail, and I went back to Rochester with suntans. The overly protective Mrs. Gordon went back to Brooklyn with overly protected sons.

I returned to play for Rochester in the 1950–51 season, a year when the NBA experienced a lot of change. The Sheboygan, Waterloo, and Anderson teams had struggled to survive, but their small town populations were too much of a handicap. It was becoming clearer that little cities in the NBA would soon be a thing of the past. The Denver franchise also collapsed, because travel there was a bitch, leaving the league with no teams west of Minneapolis. St. Louis, Chicago, and the Washington Caps disbanded, leaving only Boston, New York, and Philadelphia remaining from the original BAA.

Comings and goings in those early NBA years made for interesting developments. Teams picking up players from franchises that went out of business were able to go from also-ran to contender in one season. The Boston Celtics that year picked up two future Hall of Famers—one who they wanted and one they were stuck with. Boston was happy when it landed Easy Ed Macauley in the dispersal draft of St. Louis players. They were less happy in the dispersal draft of Chicago, ending up with a guy who had played in their own backyard at Holy Cross, a player they passed over in the regular draft. His name was Bob Cousy, and that guy became one of the top draws and greatest players in Celtic history. One thing that hasn't changed in my five decades in the NBA: any kind of drafting is a kind of crap shoot—you win some and you lose some. And sometimes you hit the jackpot.

That same year, 1950–51, blacks played in the NBA for the first time. The Celtics drafted Chuck Cooper out of Duquesne, and the Knicks signed twenty-eight-year-old Nat "Sweetwater" Clifton, a strong, showman type who had starred for the Harlem Globetrotters. Jackie Robinson went through hell breaking baseball's color line in 1947, but Cooper and Clifton had few problems in the NBA. Maybe it was because the game was so physically demanding that guys used up their aggression on the court. Whatever it was, nobody made a big deal about breaking the NBA color line. We all just kept on playing.

In those early days of the NBA, some games put people to sleep. At Minneapolis on November 22, 1950, Fort Wayne beat the Lakers, 19–18, in the lowest scoring game in NBA history. Just 31 shots were taken by both teams, which was an example of how painfully boring a stalling contest can be. That game started everyone talking about ways to prevent that kind of thing from happening.

If you've read this far in the book, you must be a real fan of basketball history. It's true, I do go back a long way in the sport, although, contrary to rumor, I wasn't the guy who held the nail when Dr. James Naismith put up the old peach basket. But I was a participant in some other basketball history, including the longest game ever played in the NBA.

On a cold night in Rochester on January 6, 1951, my Royals played against the Indianapolis Olympians in a game that droned on through six overtime periods. It was boring, boring basketball. Some of our hometown fans booed the slow motion spectacular and hundreds of others left the arena during the game. This was very unusual for Rochester, since our fans were real rooters.

The total time played—including the six overtimes—was 78 minutes. Just 23 shots were taken in the overtimes; players mainly stared at each other while one guy dribbled out the clock looking to pass for a good percentage shot. I played 76 of the total 78 minutes, and although I was in great shape, my tail was dragging when that historic marathon ended.

Great rivalries bring a lot of excitement to sports. People still talk about the old Brooklyn Dodger–New York Giant battles. Whenever the Boston Red Sox and New York Yankees clash, there's something special going on. The Knicks and Celtics have a thing going. In its own way the rivalry between my Rochester Royals and the Minneapolis Lakers was unique too. Memories of playing against the Lakers still send shivers through me.

Most of the time when I played for the Rochester Royals we would come into Minneapolis by train. Les Harrison would wrap himself up in a long scarf and big coat and jump onto the platform.

"C'mon fellas," he'd say, "it's only a ten-block walk to the hotel. We don't need cabs. The walk will invigorate you. It's cold but it's a dry cold. You'll never feel it." Les had come a long way from the days of offering all we could eat.

"It's freezing, Les," some of the guys would protest. "You're not going to feel the cold, it's dry. Believe me," Les argued. "The walk will be good for all of us. You'll feel refreshed."

We would start the walk—some might have called it a forced march. The smoke from our breath would form strange shapes in the sub-freezing air. The last few blocks of the walk would always turn into a brisk trot.

When we finally made it into the warmth of the Nicolette Hotel and thawed out, I'd realize what Les meant when he talked about not feeling a dry cold. Your ears could fall off but the rest of you would never know it.

What was becoming an annual Minneapolis ritual began again as my Rochester team faced the Lakers in the 1950–51 Western Division playoffs. They were bigger, stronger, and had the home court edge, so a lot of people were writing off our chances. Yet, we had a few things going for us—good role players, experience, and balanced scoring.

Arnie Risen, Bobby Wanzer, Bob Davies, and Jack Coleman all averaged in double figures that season. Coleman, a raw-boned man from Bergen, Kentucky, was a fine outside shooter, and a smart rebounder and passer who fit nicely with our kind of team. Les fit me in as a kind of relief pitcher, using me off the bench.

Arnie Johnson was another asset. His real name was Arnitz but nobody dared call him that. Arnie had played his college ball at Bemidji State in Minnesota—where they have a statue of Paul Bunyan on the campus. Les had sent Arnie money to take a train down to Rochester. Since Arnie didn't know if he'd get any more money, he saved what he had by coming down on the back of a milk truck all the way from Minnesota. Although Arnie was fast for a six five, 240-pound man, Les Harrison was not too impressed at first with his basketball ability and was going to release Arnie. But all the players on the Royals liked Arnie and thought he had good potential.

"Keep the big guy," I told Les. "All of us will help to teach him the ropes."

I guess that's another way the game has changed—and maybe the world has changed. Back then you'd help a guy to make your team even though you might be helping him take your place one day.

Secretly maybe some of us wanted Arnie around, thinking he'd protect us from some of the brutes on the other teams. We tried to get him to be our enforcer, but that was all we could do—try.

"He starts with me," Arnie would say in a serious voice, "I'll take care of him."

"You big son of a bitch," I'd yell at Arnie. "Who's gonna ever start with you? It's the guys that start with us that we're worried about."

We lost the first game of the playoffs to Minneapolis, and our dressing room scene before the second game was gloomy. We were always a disciplined team but had played sloppily in that first game, and the memory of a defeat like that stays with you awhile.

"I got an idea," Les Harrison told the team. "Tonight I'm gonna make a change in our starting lineup. The only time we beat Minneapolis at home this season was when I started Red against them. I'm doing that again!"

I was kind of surprised, but the switch didn't bother me any. I liked playing under pressure and was flattered to be given the responsibility of starting.

Outside of the Minneapolis State Armory it was cold and snowy, but inside there was a standing room only crowd—hot and howling for the Lakers.

"Don't worry about scoring, Red," Les told me just before we took the floor. "Just control things. Quiet the team down."

I was prepared to do what Les told me to (I always listened to the coach). But I got off hot. I got the feel of it. I hit my first couple of long two-hand set shots and I knew I couldn't miss. I played the whole game, which was tough since I hadn't had all that much playing time during the year. I was a little arm and leg weary hitting ten of 13 from the field and wound up with 23 points, high for both teams. All my points came off Slater Martin, the best defensive guard in the league, and I held him to just two points. In the fourth quarter I didn't shoot at all but concentrated on protecting our slight lead.

We won the game by four points and I was lit up. I'd had my greatest performance in what turned out to be the most important game I ever played in my life, the most important game the Rochester Royals ever played. The momentum carried us past Minneapolis into the NBA championship finals.

A year later and we were back. This time it was April 21, 1951—a Saturday—the first time in NBA history that the championship series came down to the seventh game: the New York Knickerbockers against my Rochester Royals.

We had flown back and forth between Rochester and New York City on an old DC-3 prop plane in the first six games of the championship series with the Knicks. The media milked the match-up—the smaller upstate city of Rochester versus the powerful urban center of New York City. It did a lot to help publicize the NBA.

Our fans at the Edgerton Park Arena were usually loud, but I never heard them roar like they did in that seventh game. With seconds left in the first half, I hit a set shot to give us a six-point lead. And with less than a minute left in the game I was dribbling the ball, killing the clock, protecting our two-point lead, listening to the clamor of the crowd.

It was an incredible thrill for me, for all the Royals, to be on an NBA championship team, to win the title before our hometown fans.

That was the greatest moment in the history of Rochester sports, and the people in the city celebrated all that spring and throughout the summer. Selma, Gail, and I celebrated right along with them.

On October 19, 1951, the eve of the new season, the young National Basketball Association was given a jolt. Ralph Beard and Alex Groza of the Indianapolis Olympians, two of the big stars in the league, were picked up on charges that they had been involved in fixing games when they played at the University of Kentucky. As NBA champions my Rochester team had played a 1951–52 pre-season exhibition tour against the Indianapolis Olympians. We had moved from city to city with them and the fans loved the intensely competitive level of play. The only nagging thing was that some strangers who didn't seem to be basketball fans were always hanging around.

Those strangers were law officials who picked up Groza and Beard when our exhibition game ended. Beard and Groza were never allowed to play in the NBA again. The guys on my Rochester team were shocked by the whole thing.

What happened with Beard and Groza disillusioned some fans. Others thought those guys were treated too harshly, being barred for life. But more than anything else, it showed how concerned the NBA has always been about any kind of scandal—knowing that if fans lose faith in the honesty of the game, there would be no game. I always felt sad that Ralph Beard and Alex Groza ended that way, because they could have gone on to become all-time greats.

Always looking for ways to safeguard and improve its product, the NBA that 1951–52 season widened the free throw lane—where an offensive player can't stay for more than three seconds—from six to 12 feet. With the lane's width doubled, George Mikan and other giants would have less space close to the basket to work from. A pivot player now would have to take an extra step wheeling in for a shot. The alley was also opened up more for driving, and the defensive teams had a better chance for a rebound.

Mikan was such a great player that the rule didn't hamper him much. Second in league scoring that season, George led his Lakers to victory over my Rochester team in the divisional final.

That season the NBA had much more stability. You didn't need a roadmap to keep up with the teams. There was only one franchise shift—Ben Kerner moved his Tri Cities Blackhawks to Milwaukee, a shift which would affect me later on.

Winding up my ninth pro season, I looked around, and a lot of the teams, coaches, and players I had started out with were gone. The style of the game had changed a lot from the days when I had worn leather knee guards with felt linings to protect myself against floor burns.

I was thirty-two years old with a lot of wear and tear on my body, a lot of playing time behind me. And although my whole life had been nothing but basketball, I was starting to wonder about what to do with the rest of it.

That summer of 1953 I was relaxing with Selma and Gail in Long Beach when the phone rang. "Hey, champ. How you doing?"

It was my buddy Fuzzy Levane, who was about to begin his second season coaching the Milwaukee Hawks. After we swapped some basketball gossip, Fuzz popped the question.

"How'd you like to play for me with Milwaukee?"

"I don't have that much left, Fuzzy. Besides, I'm happy in Rochester."

"Red, you don't have to tell me you don't have that much left— I've seen you play. But you got enough for what I want. All you'll do is handle the ball a little bit and help me keep the cows I have here moving."

"I don't know." I stalled Fuzzy. I really didn't.

"C'mon, Red. I need someone in Milwaukee to share the misery with me. I need someone whose chops I can bust, someone I can trust. Help me out."

"Okay, okay, Fuzzy. I'm yours."

I had some misgivings about leaving Rochester, having established a home there and a lot of good friends. Yet, I was winding down with the Royals. And it was logical for me to move on.

Fuzzy Levane took his job as Milwaukee coach very seriously. In our training camp we had two-a-day workouts. As promised, he busted our chops—and I was moaning from all the aches and pains.

"Is this any way to treat a friend?" I asked Fuzz.

"It's the best way I know, Red," he answered. "These workouts will add years to your career."

"These workouts will kill me first."

After the training camp ended, we staged a two-week exhibition tour throughout the Midwest against my old rivals, the Minneapolis Lakers. Games were played in high school and college gyms in places like Bemidji State (Arnie Johnson's alma mater), Iron City, Michigan, Kalamazoo—freezing places, but the locals there walked around in undershirts.

Our team would have had trouble beating anybody. Here we were matched up against the world champions—a team with George Mikan, Vern Mikkelsen, Jim Pollard, Slater Martin, Clyde Lovellette. We were the cannon fodder for the great Minneapolis Lakers and it showed. They toyed with us throughout the tour. We played twelve games. We lost twelve games.

In those early years of the National Basketball Association most teams were owned by individuals, not wealthy corporations. Some teams lived from payday to payday, from season to season. And owners like Milwaukee's Ben Kerner did whatever was necessary to stay in business.

Out of 30 scheduled home games that season, we played 14 at home. The other games were on the road against NBA teams, and we shared the billing with the Harlem Globetrotters. Ben Kerner netted about $5,000 for each of those games and saved a lot of money by not having to open the Milwaukee arena.

Kerner also sold two of our better players to bring in some cash. Jack Nichols went to Boston for $15,000 and Mel Hutchins to Fort Wayne for $25,000. It doesn't seem like a lot of money today, and wasn't even that much money back in those days, but the forty grand helped keep Ben Kerner and the Milwaukee Hawks in business for another season.

Fuzzy was let go after the team won just 11 of its first 46 games. I felt bad for Fuzzy, but that was the breaks of the game. He knew it and I knew it.

Ben Kerner appointed me coach of the Hawks. I was just past 33 at the time—a little young for coaching. In one day I went from playing with those guys to coaching them. In a sense it was on-the-job training and I had to use all of my native smarts to get by. I had to learn what to do by eliminating things I shouldn't be doing. And I did a lot of eliminating. We finished the year in last place in the Western Division, 25 games behind the Minneapolis Lakers. I seemed to be making a career out of chasing that damn team.

My only consolation was that the Hawks won ten of the last 26 games I coached. No big deal, but given the talent we had that was progress.

The way the season ended showed the financial condition our team was in. We were scheduled to play Baltimore at home in Milwaukee on the last day of the season and then go to Baltimore for the final game for both teams. Those games meant nothing, since both teams were in the cellar. Eager to save a little money, Ben Kerner convinced Baltimore's management to play both games in Milwaukee. I believe that's the only time in NBA history that the same two teams played each other in a doubleheader. We beat Baltimore in both games, and I was the star in each game.

That summer I hooked up with the Harlem Globetrotters for a two-week tour playing basketball in major league baseball parks when the home team was on the road.

Goose Tatum, the star of the Globies, was an incredible showman with all kinds of rubbery moves and great athletic ability. About six three and very lanky, Tatum was all elbows and joints playing with a ball and using his extra long 84-inch reach for gags. The "Goose" had an amazing hook shot that he threw up from any angle, and he usually made a basket. Wearing an old slouch hat, faking guys out of their jocks—the Goose was as funny as any clown.

However, when he left the floor, Tatum went through a transformation, becoming introverted and quiet. His sadness away from the basketball court and the spotlight made an impression on me.

As the star of the Globetrotters, Goose got around in his big white Cadillac. It was summertime, hot as hell, and the guys on the Globetrotters always battled to ride with him and get into that air-conditioning. Goose was always agreeable, on one condition. They all had to sit in the front, and one guy had to drive. Nobody sat in the back of that big white Cadillac but Goose.

After a few days of the tour had passed, I noticed the Globetrotters constantly arguing among themselves before a game. My name was always part of the debate.

"You had him last night—you can't have him again tonight—it's not fair," one guy would bitch. "I gotta guard Holzman. I gotta get some rest tonight."

"How much do you want? I'll pay you. Let me guard that old Holzman," another guy would yell back.

"No way," a third guy would cut in. "You both can't have him. We rotate him, and that gives Holzman to me."

I had planned on playing one more season with the Hawks, especially after my smashing finish in the doubleheader against Baltimore, but overhearing the Globetrotters argue over who was going to guard me, I knew I was done.

My pro playing career came to an end just as that of one of the all-time greats began. Bob Pettit, our number one draft choice out of Louisiana State University, joined the Hawks for the 1954–55 season.

Bob's first game was against the defending champion Minneapolis Lakers in a high school gymnasium in Wolf Point, Montana. The Lakers kicked his butt in the first half. They just manhandled him.

"Bob," I asked during halftime, "do you enjoy being a professional basketball player?"

"Yeah, coach," he said. "I like it just fine. I'm having a real good time."

All the time I coached Pettit I rarely yelled at him, but that night I knew a little something extra was called for.

"Bob, if you don't hit the first guy you come up against when the second half begins," I yelled, "then I'm gonna ship you back to Baton Rouge, Louisiana where you came from. If you don't show some aggressiveness, those guys on the other team will wipe the floor with you."

The second half began, and I knew that Pettit was looking to make contact with the smallest guy he could find. He found one in Slater Martin, five ten, 165 pounds. Pettit swung an elbow. Martin ducked his head. Pettit's elbow smashed into the chest of big, burly Vern Mikkelsen, one of the toughest characters around.

Pettit hadn't planned it that way, but he had sent a message that he couldn't be intimidated—and the message got around the league.

Pettit was six nine, 215 pounds, mobile, a great shooter with terrific range. I switched him from the center position he was used to and made him a big forward. Bob was a finesse forward—not that quick, but like Larry Bird, he knew how to get to the right spot at the right time. I spent long hours teaching Bob to shoot facing the basket instead of with his back to it, and his shooting got better and better as he developed confidence.

I always called him "Schlim," meaning slim, but though Bob looked thin, he was powerful and had a lot of stamina. In 72 games and 2,659 minutes, a lot of minutes, Bob averaged 20.4 points a game and was voted Rookie of the Year. Later Pettit became the first player in NBA history to score more than 20,000 points in a career.

A player with great pride and a great heart, Pettit was the franchise for the Hawks, always wanting the ball when the game was on the line. He was also unselfish and intelligent and gave up the ball when he had to. Like Bill Bradley, Bob had a knack for getting along with everybody; he drove an old used car and never put on airs.

Even with Bob Pettit and Frank Selvy, who averaged 19 points a game, our team struggled on the court and at the gate. The Boston Braves had moved to Milwaukee, and the fans were interested in seeing top baseball more than mediocre basketball. I tried to rally our players with what became my famous clubhouse meeting talk.

"Fellows—it's nice to have you all here in the same place listening to your coach," I began. "Although things haven't been going that great for our club, I know all of you can dig down deeper and play a little more skillfully."

Some of them would nod their heads, while others would come up with the lip-biting expression that was meant to show me they were determined.

I would then stop my little speech and make a big thing out of reaching into my pants pocket and digging out my wallet. I opened my wallet and very tenderly pulled out a photograph of my little daughter, Gail.

"You see this sweet little kid, guys," I would emote. "She's beautiful and I love her. She likes to eat, like all kids do. But if we don't win some more games and make some more money for the organization, she's gonna just waste away."

The speech wasn't exactly Knute Rockne's "Win One for the

Gipper." It didn't have the same effect either, but we won five more games that 1954–55 season than we had the year before. With my old pal Al Cervi coaching them and Dolph Schayes leading the way, Syracuse won its first and only NBA championship that season. That Syracuse team was also the first NBA champion with black players on it, Earl Lloyd and Jim Tucker. The league kept on changing.

One of the biggest changes was the creation of the 24-second rule mandating that a player shoot within that time limit.

In 1951, when I had been playing for Rochester, Les Harrison took me along to an NBA owner's meeting as an observer. The problem of stalling was discussed and the six-overtime game I had played in was cited as an example.

"It might not be a bad idea," I said to the owners, "for some kind of shot clock to be used."

"You concentrate on playing the game, Red," one of the owners snapped. Somehow I got the distinct impression that they saw me as a young squirt. They went on with their discussions, and I went back to my observing.

Danny Biasone, owner of Syracuse, came up with the specifics of the 24-second clock, and he sold it to the other owners. In 1954–55, his Nats won the championship, benefiting from the clock with their team's quick running game and strong defensive rebounding.

The effect of the 24-second clock became clear in its first season. Scoring jumped to 93.1 points a team, an increase of almost 15 points a team.

The 24-second clock revolutionized pro basketball, changing it from a defensive to an offensive game. No longer could players stand around and stall, not with the pressure of the clock. Ironically, the clock also improved defense because teams worked the clock to make the offensive team take a poor percentage shot.

Outlet passes, fast breaks, posting up guys, dribbling, and running skills became more important. The game became more athletically demanding and a lot of the old rough and tumble tactics disappeared. Coaching philosophies were also changed by the 24-second clock. Coaches told their teams to get the ball up court in a couple of seconds to gain more time to work the ball in a half court offense. The 24-second rule was a great innovation that opened up the game and excited the fans.

With or without a clock, fans were something we were seeing less of in Milwaukee, so Ben Kerner moved the team to St. Louis for the 1955–56 season. Our arrival was a shot in the arm for civic pride, because the year before, baseball's St. Louis Browns had moved out to Baltimore. Some criticized Kerner because of his move to St. Louis, but he was a shrewd businessman who picked up the largest population in the NBA Western Division to draw from.

One way he saved money was on payroll. I remember when Marty Blake, today the head of NBA scouting, was hired by Kerner as publicity man for the Hawks. I was alone in the locker room when Kerner brought Blake in to show him around.

"Red, I'm really excited about starting a new season with you as coach." Blake was kind of hyper. "Could you introduce me to the rest of the staff?"

I grabbed him by his shoulder and turned him around to face a mirror. "You see those three guys?" Ben, Blake, and I were the three guys in the mirror. "That's the staff, Marty!"

Bob Pettit came into his own that season, leading the league in scoring. And Kerner picked up thirty-seven-year-old Alex Hannum to bolster the troops. We were starting to get a good nucleus of players, but guys were still coming and going.

One night the team was on the road and I was in my hotel room relaxing and watching a movie with horses in it. The phone rang.

"Red, Red!" It was Ben Kerner. "I'm calling to tell you to get rid of player X." (I'm not putting the guy's name in here to protect the guilty.) "There's no need for us to keep him on the roster," Kerner continued. "Call him in and tell him he's through with the Hawks."

I knew that I was going to be in for a tough time. Player X was six ten, about 250 pounds, strong and nasty. I called him on the phone and told him to come to my room for an important announcement.

"I'll be right there," he barked.

I had it all planned out. I'd make some small talk and then let player X down gently. I would also try to keep out of his punching range, which I knew would be tough. My room was economy size.

After the preliminaries were concluded I began the real business. "I got a call from the front office today," I spoke softly. "We have to make some changes on the team . . . we are going to have to let you go. It's not my idea, but I've gotta give you the message."

Player X was quiet for a couple of moments. Then he bellowed. "You mother f-----." He was wild. "Coach, you gonna let me go and keep that old mother f-----, Hannum." (He was referring to Alex Hannum, a veteran, but not a mother f-----.) "How can you keep that old man and cut me?"

Backed up against the door, I think I spoke calmly. "It wasn't my idea. If it was up to me, I'd keep you, you show a lot of potential. The whole idea came from management."

With my sweaty hand I held on to the doorknob in case I was forced to make an emergency exit. Player X kept shouting and coming closer, and my economy-size room had started to shrink to almost closet size when I finally managed to finish with him, push the door open, and send him on his way. I was happy knowing that I would be able to go on with my life—which had just started passing before my eyes.

That experience—the first time I ever cut a player—taught me a lesson: never release a guy in a small room; always do it in an open area—a dance floor, a gym, a football field. Seriously, though, cutting a player is a job that has to be done by somebody, and through the years I was given that unpleasant job many times. I always tried not to hurt a guy's ego and was careful to say positive things. I would also always tell a guy face-to-face that he was going to be cut, and I'd make a sincere effort to help him get a job somewhere else.

We finished the 1955–56 season tied with Minneapolis for second place in our division. The Lakers had started poorly that season, so George Mikan, who had retired and become general manager, returned to help his team. With the 24-second clock, the added movement on the floor, and his age, it was no longer Mikan's game. It was sad to see an all-time great like George come back and not perform up to his former high standards.

I sometimes wonder what it would have been like to have coached Bill Russell, and I almost had the chance. Russell had starred for the

University of San Francisco and for the United States basketball team in the 1956 Olympics in Melbourne. Kerner drafted Bill and then traded him because Ben didn't have the money to sign Russell. That's how the Boston Celtics wound up with one of the greatest players of all time and the Hawks obtained Ed Macauley and former Kentucky All-American Cliff Hagan.

I tried Hagan at the guard spot but saw that was not his position. I realized that since Cliff had such a great hook shot and was sturdy, the forward position would be best for him. It took some time for me to build Cliff's confidence and develop his outside shooting, but once that was accomplished he became basketball's first great small forward and a perfect complement to Pettit, whose inside game made up for Cliff's lack of size and rebounding.

We acquired Slater Martin from Minneapolis, and with Pettit, Macauley, and Hagan on the roster, Kerner felt 1956–57 was "the year of the St. Louis Hawks." It was becoming my kind of team—a mix of veterans and younger guys. I attempted to instill the techniques I had picked up from my days at CCNY and Rochester—team offense, team defense, moving the ball, hitting the open man, role playing, lots of repetition. I let the players know their roles, what their jobs were, when they'd play, and how to fit in with Pettit, who was the main man.

By mid-season we couldn't quite get it all together—maybe because there were a lot of new parts to fit in. The team's record was 14–19 when Kerner let me go. Slater Martin replaced me as coach and then Alex Hannum replaced Slater.

Hannum won just five more games than I did, but coached St. Louis to victory in the Western Division playoffs. In the championship series Alex brought the Hawks to the final seconds of the seventh game against the Boston Celtics before losing. The next year, with the nucleus of players I had left behind, the Hawks won the NBA championship.

I never second-guessed Kerner when he replaced me. The Hawks weren't doing that poorly, and I felt that I was developing a potential for a championship team, that it was just a matter of time. . . . But Kerner expected more out of that team than 14–19.

It wasn't easy. It even stung a little for me to see the team I left win the NBA championship a couple of years later, but Hannum and

Kerner did a great job developing the nucleus I left behind on the Hawks. And Ben Kerner did a great deal for pro basketball. He was one of the pioneers along with Les Harrison, Eddie Gottlieb, and the others. I believe that Kerner belongs with the other pioneers in the Basketball Hall of Fame.

I collected my salary for the rest of the 1956–57 season from the Hawks. It was strange being out of basketball, but it felt good to relax and unwind at home, which was now in Cedarhurst, Long Island. Selma, Gail, and I had moved back to the New York City area while I was coaching the St. Louis Hawks. Selma had lost her dad around that time and she wanted to live closer to her mother and her sister, Roslyn.

Losing the job as coach of the Hawks had rattled my confidence and started me thinking of other careers, other things aside from basketball.

Fuzzy Levane, who had become Knick scout, wouldn't let me stay away from basketball, however. "Red," he said, "you know more about the game than most coaches in the league. C'mon. Come down to the Garden. Be seen. We'll find a way for you to get back into basketball."

Grudgingly, I went to a few games, mixed with people, and bided my time. In 1958–59, Vince Boryla moved up from coaching the Knicks and became general manager. He appointed Fuzzy Levane coach. And once again Fuzzy delivered for me. He told Vince he wanted me for chief scout.

An original thinker and an outspoken guy, Vince is a respected man in basketball. I had only a nodding kind of relationship with him at that time, but he went along with Fuzzy and convinced Knick president Ned Irish to give me the job.

I actually could have been a member of the New York Knickerbocker organization way back in 1946. After my first year with Rochester, Neil Cohalan, who was preparing to coach the Knicks in their first season in the BAA, approached me.

"Ned Irish sent me to make you an offer to play for the Knicks," Cohalan said. "We like your style, Red. And you're from New York City."

"I appreciate the offer," I told Cohalan. "It would be nice to play in my hometown, but I owe Les Harrison the opportunity to match your offer. Let me talk to Les and I'll get back to you."

Les not only matched the offer but gave me a little more, and I passed up the chance to play for the Knicks.

Cohalan lasted just that first year with the Knicks because Joe Lapchick became available. A great motivator, Lapchick always got his Knick teams into the playoffs. Joe resigned during the 1955–56 season and was replaced as coach by Vince Boryla, who had starred for the team.

Now the Knick lineup for 1958–59 was Boryla as G.M., Fuzzy Levane as coach, and me as chief scout. And I was raring to go.

CHAPTER 3

I began my work as Knick scout and assistant coach on April 29, 1958. The time I had spent in Rochester, Milwaukee, and St. Louis was filled with excitement and good memories, but now I would be back working in the Big Apple, where I had grown up—and the thought of doing that was even more exciting. It was also a great feeling to be back in basketball. And although at the start my scouting would only be part-time, I built it up quite a bit, and as the league expanded so did the job.

Scouting for the Knicks would be my future for a decade. The job would shape me and I would shape the job. And although I was recommending players for different Knick coaches, I couldn't help but develop my own personal vision of the right combination of players that would make for a winning team.

Logistically, the job worked out well too. In New York, Selma was near her family, and the neighbors on the block in Cedarhurst always looked out for her and Gail while I did my scouting.

On the road I was prepared for any emergency. I always made sure I had a bottle of scotch in my bag for medicinal purposes. One of my chief props was a big raincoat with very large pockets. I moved about a lot and kept a spare shirt, a writing pad, extra socks, an extra bottle of scotch—all the comforts and necessities—in those big raincoat pockets. Through those years as chief scout I traveled about 100,000 miles a year. I made sure I saw at least one game a night—college, NBA, Eastern League, any kind of game.

The Knicks were the first franchise to go in for scouting in a serious way. When I first began I had the country all to myself. It did worry me a little because I knew I had the worst sense of direction in the world. However, I had a little trick that helped. When my instincts told me to go right I would go left, and I almost always headed in the right direction.

Sometimes I wound up with a really eerie feeling, like being in limbo, free-floating. When I finally settled down and slept a few hours, I'd get up not knowing what time zone I was in. I would open my eyes and wonder, Where the hell am I? Chicago? El Paso? I was literally wandering across America.

I traveled to some of the most scenic spots in the United States but never went out of my way to check out the sights. All I had on my mind was the best restaurant, a place to stay, and getting set for basketball. I figured that one day I could see all those places when I returned with Selma on a book tour after I wrote my autobiography.

It's lonely being on the road that much. Sometimes I ran into a guy I'd walk half a block to avoid in New York City. But off by myself in some part of Utah, coming across that familiar face, I'd throw my arms around the guy. "Hey, how ya doin'? Whatcha doin' for dinner tonight?"

I had a couple of scares along the way. In 1961 things were pretty bad in Pikeville, Kentucky when I went down there to sign Donnis Butcher, a seventh round draft pick for the Knicks.

"You know, Mr. Holzman, there's so much poverty here now that people would shoot you in five seconds for that raincoat you're wearing," Butcher told me.

We stayed up talking until about five in the morning in a hotel that must have been 300 years old. Roach races were going on in the room as we talked, trying to figure out if Butcher should sign with the Knicks—and how he could get me out of Pikeville with my coat and my life.

Once I was driving a rented car in Alabama. It started pouring like hell. The car gave out somewhere between Reform and Gordo. I wound up in some little motel-boarding house. It rained all night and the ceiling leaked in my room. The next morning the guy who ran the motel told me that if I hurried I could catch up with some guys who could give me a lift to Tuscaloosa. I ran like hell and jumped into a beat-up pickup truck. There were two guys in it—tough-looking characters. They both needed a shave and they wore overalls that had seen better times.

We drove out. I tried to make conversation.

"You guys like basketball?"

"Crap sport," one of them snapped.

I decided to stay quiet for the rest of the trip.

We had driven about a half an hour when the guy who didn't like basketball made like he was on the Indianapolis Speedway, pulled the pickup off the side of the road, and drove it into the woods down a dirt path. Boy, I figured, I'm in trouble. There goes my raincoat and maybe me.

As it turned out, they had made a detour to pick up another guy, who looked even meaner. He slid into his seat in the truck and gave me a scowl. I made believe I didn't notice. He got to talking to the other guys only after we were driving for ten minutes. It turned out they were giving him a lift to Tuscaloosa too. It was only when I heard that that I decided to wipe the cold sweat off my brow. Just another day on the road as a scout.

Colleges I visited were like separate countries with a lot of local pride. Although some coaches exaggerated a player's ability, others were honest almost to a fault. I learned how to evaluate what the coaches said as well as some of the things they left unsaid.

Initially, I was the only scout at some of the black colleges. A Navy buddy of mine, Red Thomas, a professor at Northwestern State University, opened the door for me at those places. One thing led to another and I became pretty friendly with the people in charge there. I would visit Winston-Salem, Grambling, Norfolk, Jackson State, Little Rock—great basketball schools, but ironically their athletic programs were hurt when the doors were opened and all the good players went off to bigger schools.

Most colleges allowed me to sit at the press table, but at some places, the cozy ones, I preferred to sit in the stands, out of the limelight. It was more comfortable for me and made for better concentration.

I corresponded with people all over the world—other scouts, former players, sportswriters, coaches. You'd get a good report, you'd check it out. If you liked what you saw, you'd check still further.

I also mailed forms to college seniors after the season asking for their height and weight, military status, plans for graduate or professional school. The form would ask players to list position played, best shot, team defense. I'd also ask them to name a few of the best college players they played against. It was like an insurance company letter—name three guys we can call. If a player named guys we hadn't heard about, we'd check them out too. The form would also ask about other sports played, and if they wanted to play for the Knicks.

At Indiana I scouted Dick and Tom Van Arsdale, the twins. They played a similar style of basketball, and it was difficult to tell them apart. Scouting them reminded me of a story from the old neighborhood.

When a Jewish person died, a guy was hired to sit in the funeral home and watch the body. An old man in the neighborhood was called "the watcher," and for ten dollars he would stay up all night in the funeral home and watch over the body.

One night he reported for work and noticed that there were two bodies.

"I want twenty dollars," he complained to the funeral home owner. "There are two bodies to watch."

The owner pointed to one of the bodies. "Just watch him, forget about the other guy—he won't ever know the difference."

That was the way it was with me and Dick and Tom Van Arsdale. When they played, I watched just one. The other Van Arsdale never knew the difference.

When draft time came it was tough choosing between Dick and Tom. I thought Dick was just a little better foul shooter and a little stronger defensively than Tom, so I recommended him, and the Knicks signed him. However, they were both outstanding players and people and had fine professional careers.

No matter where you go as a scout, it's easy to spot the best player. The trick is to take a player out of his environment and imagine him in the pros. Is the player good just because he's on a college team? Will he get any better? Scouting always leaves you open for mistakes. You have to evaluate for potential: size for position, ability for position, ability for another position.

I always looked to see if a player wanted the ball when the game was on the line, or if he scored his points when it was garbage time— after the game was decided and the points meant nothing. I was always concerned about guts, attitude, intelligence, unselfishness.

Players would come into the NBA from college where they'd been hot dogs, and they had to learn to fit in. They had to learn that life didn't revolve around them, that sacrificing for the team, a big part of basketball, was needed. For some that didn't come easy, and there were others who could never learn it. I tried hard to find out how willing players were to sacrifice for a team.

All scouting accomplishes something; you're never wasting time. If nothing else, I would wind up eliminating players, and that in itself was doing something—by not doing something.

My first year as a scout, Fuzzy's first year as Knick head coach, the team finished in second place. I always thought Fuzzy did a great job, but he really didn't have much talent to work with aside from Richie Guerin and Carl Braun. Willie Naulls was getting started and Frank Selvy was finishing up, but Fuzzy was able to get a lot of mileage out of everybody.

That year was Elgin Baylor's first as a pro. A shot in the arm for the Minneapolis Lakers, fourth in scoring in the league, Baylor became only the third rookie up to then to make the all-NBA team. Bob Pettit won the MVP award and was second in the league in rebounding and third in scoring.

However, the dominant force in the NBA was the Boston Celtics— winning their second NBA championship in three years on their way to a string of eight straight titles. All the time I scouted for the Knicks, the Celtics kept on winning. They are still the only true dynasty in NBA history, and all those banners in Boston Garden never let you forget it.

If there's anyone close to a genius in basketball, it has to be Red

Auerbach. He did a tremendous job getting the players, coaching
them, and keeping them in line within his system. And when Red got
Bill Russell, he knew what to do with him.

Teams had fast breaks before Russell, but with him the Celtics
transformed that part of the game, creating their offense through
Russell's defense. With Bill getting the ball to them, the Celtics were
able to beat other teams down the floor. His shot blocking was aimed
not at batting the ball out of bounds, but at getting it to one of his
teammates. It all fit into one system under Red Auerbach.

The Celtics had a great nucleus through those years of their
dynasty: Bob Cousy, Bill Sharman, Frank Ramsey, K. C. Jones, Sam
Jones, Tommy Heinsohn, John Havlicek. And as guys left, they added
a player here and there. And they gave him time to fit in.

The opposite situation existed with the Knicks. Aside from Fuzzy's
second place finish, all those early Knick teams wound up in last place
in the Eastern Division. And that made it tough for the Knick coaches
and the players that were drafted.

Ned Irish ran everything that had to do with the New York
Knickerbockers along with his assistant, Freddy Podesta. Irish was
aloof, but he was a real basketball fan. If he had a fault, it was that he
was perhaps too much of a fan, and sometimes that seemed to
influence his hiring and firing.

Fuzzy Levane was let go as coach during the 1959–60 season and
replaced by Carl Braun, one of the great players in Knickerbocker
history. Like all great players, Carl had some trouble coaching because
he expected others to do things as easily and as well as he had done
them. Maybe that's why fringe players often have better success as
coaches than great players. The former great players expect their teams
to perform as well as they once did, and they get frustrated when their
players don't perform at that level. But generally, fringe players who
go on to coach are naturally a bit more patient.

If the 1960 draft rules had been the way they are today, we would
have been faced with the awesome responsibility of choosing between
Oscar Robertson and Jerry West. But draft rules back then allowed
Cincinnati to acquire Robertson as a territorial choice. The Lakers,
who had moved to Los Angeles, making the league truly national, had
finished third in the West the year before. Their record, however, was

two games worse than the Knicks, who finished fourth, so they picked ahead of us and took Jerry West.

Years of last-place finishes by the Knicks had made the organization and the fans hungry for a player to come in and turn things around, but unless you're drafting a Jerry West, an Oscar Robertson, or a Bill Russell, players need time to develop. I was working to get the Knick organization to go for the best player available in the draft instead of going for a big center who might turn things around and be an immediate franchise saver.

Our 1960 top draft pick was Darrall Imhoff, and in addition to being six ten and a center, he was also a logical choice for us. Darrall had starred at the University of California, which won the NCAA title under Coach Pete Newell. Unfortunately, Imhoff played only two years for the Knicks—two years with a lot of pressure on him. And not everybody can play or coach in New York with that much pressure on him.

Part of the reason for the Knicks to sign up a big center was all those years of losing records and last-place finishes. Another part was the play of Bill Russell in Boston and Wilt Chamberlain in Philadelphia. Wilt joined the Warriors in 1959–60. One of the greatest athletes of all time—a one-man basketball record book, Chamberlain was a shot blocker, a rebounder, and a pretty good shooter. He could do anything he put his mind to on the court except shoot fouls. One year he led the league in assists simply because he made up his mind he was going to.

In the 1961–62 season Eddie Donovan came from St. Bonaventure College to coach the Knicks, replacing Carl Braun. The year before, the team had the worst record in the NBA, its sixth last-place finish in seven years.

Since the Knicks had the worst record in the league, we expected to get Walt Bellamy of Indiana in the draft. He was a mobile six-ten center and everyone's dream draft pick, but the NBA owners awarded the right to select him to the new Chicago franchise.

Ned Irish was very upset by the whole thing, and justifiably so. Walt Bellamy went on to win the Rookie of the Year award, but even with him Chicago was only 18–62. Bellamy hadn't helped Chicago that much, but he would have been a real boon to the Knicks. And having Bellamy in New York City would have also helped the league with media exposure and publicity.

Through all my years of scouting, whenever decisions were made as to whom to draft, they always came out in the press as an organizational decision, a "we" thing. "We" meant me, whoever the coach and general manager were at the time, and Ned Irish. With a strong general manager, Irish's veto power was diminished, but he always had the final say.

Different coaches, systems, and players moving in and out didn't make much difference to me in my job. I was out there scouting and recruiting for probably the best franchise in the league. We played in the greatest building with the greatest history with the greatest fans and all types of media coverage. The Knicks always went first class and treated me well, and I just went about my job looking for the best players I could find to help build the Knicks through the draft.

My time as chief Knick scout was pretty hectic, but I was able to take it easy during the summers when I was off. In 1963 my friend, Dick Isaacs, whose family had been in business in Puerto Rico for forty years, told me about an opening for a coach with the Ponce team of the Puerto Rican Summer League, who played basketball from the end of June to September.

I had never been to Puerto Rico, but I knew that top coaches like Jack Ramsey, Tex Winters, Jack McKinney, and later Paul Westhead had coached at Ponce. I talked it over with Selma and we decided to give Puerto Rico a try.

My first weeks on the job were spent practicing with the players at night on a court laid out on a baseball park infield. No lights were on in the stands since it was a practice, but I knew people were there. They didn't make any noise, but I could see the glow of the cigarettes and cigars they were smoking. It was kind of an eerie feeling—all those reddish glows and puffs of smoke in the darkness.

You couldn't expect things to run like clockwork in Puerto Rico because players came from different time zones. I'd call a practice for six or seven o'clock and expect everybody on the team to attend. At times three guys, four guys would show up and I would work with them. If just one guy showed for practice, I'd work with the one guy.

After a few good sessions of practice I was getting a pretty good feel for the situation. The players were willing to learn, and the atmosphere was pleasant. Then I was told that Willie Vicens wanted to talk to me privately about an urgent matter.

"Red," he began, "we have a problem."

"What's wrong?"

"There is an uprising by the people. The fans want to have you fired."

I was shocked. "Willie, I don't think I've done anything wrong yet. Give me a chance to screw things up before you fire me."

"Red, I am sorry," he said. "You're not making a good impression on the people. They have watched your practices. They do not think that you are a real coach."

I was dumbfounded. "How come?"

"Red, you do not use a clipboard. The people here have seen many coaches, but they have never seen a coach without a clipboard. They think you are not a real coach."

In all my coaching experience I had never used a clipboard. I explained that I preferred to concentrate on the game, not on pieces of paper, and Willie understood. He asked the fans to be patient, telling them that someone who had coached in the NBA was good enough to coach in Ponce.

The incident with the clipboard showed just how wrapped up the fans there were in the game of basketball. They were fanatically loyal to their town teams and incredibly emotional. Fans threw eggs, tomatoes, and all kinds of junk onto the court. In a few places, a fish-net-type arrangement was installed around the court to protect the players from rabid fans but sometimes that didn't do much good. Some guys could throw an egg forty feet through a hole in the net and hit their mark. I coached in games when it took us almost two hours to make it out of the place—and that was *with* a police escort.

The level of play was equivalent to good small-time college basketball. Games were played according to international rules, and I used a lot of zones and freezes. At times I experimented and learned through trial and error what worked and what was lousy. It was a tremendous learning experience. I became accustomed to all types of defenses, approaches to the game, personalities.

The teams were an amalgamation of all types. You could find an engineer, a doctor, a thirty-five-year-old businessman, or a kid from the hills. On my Ponce Leones (*Leones* is Spanish for "lions"), I had some great guys. Angel Garcia was a likable university student, always being kidded by the other players about his failing grades. Today he is a college professor. Salvatore Dijols was always under a tree taking a snooze, never in a hurry to do anything, but he was a fine, natural talent. His name was pronounced "deehorse." To my English ear it sounded like "the horse." Cesar Bocachica, our six-two center, was an engineering student at Mayaguez.

In my first year at Ponce I got my Lions into the championship against a team coached by Lou Rossini. Bocachica missed the game because he couldn't get a flight from Mayaguez; there was a tropical rainstorm. I heard all kinds of stories about players missing games, but I never ran up against one that topped that. Closeness between coaches and players couldn't be avoided, especially when we all piled into Willie Vicens's VW bug. Willie and I sat in the front, and three players would squeeze into the back. They were small guys for basketball players, so that's not quite as intimate as it sounds.

Puerto Rican League basketball finals were staged outdoors, at Bithorn Stadium in San Juan, a baseball stadium that seated about 18,000 for basketball. They could have sold twice that number of tickets.

It rained like hell at times in the San Juan area. The rain would start and stop, start and stop. The floor would be soaked, and you'd ask for it to be swabbed and dried so you could continue the game. If we were winning against a San Juan team, the guy with the mop would be nowhere to be found. They would say that he was out to lunch or that the mops were broken. If we were losing the game, fans would leap out of the stands, tear off their shirts, and use them to start mopping up. That was the most incredible example of the home court edge I ever saw.

After we won a championship, people in Ponce would go through the streets acting crazy, having the time of their lives in one huge celebration complete with parades, banners, bands, and lots of drinking. I would finally get to bed about three in the morning, and they would still be carrying on. They'd bang on my door, yelling for me to come out and join them. I would act as if I didn't hear them, but they made such a racket that they would finally get me out of there anyway.

My experiences in Puerto Rico are among the most satisfying of my life. I made a lot of lasting friendships, with Willie, Coco, and Pachen Vicens, Arnoldo Hernandez, Fredo Toro, and many others. Not only did I learn to get along with all kinds of people, I was able to try out all kinds of basketball approaches head-to-head against some really top coaches.

The people in Puerto Rico always held me in high regard. Maybe that's because I won championships three out of four years and was smart enough to quit in a winning year. I went out on a high note.

I look back now at my summers in Puerto Rico as an all-expenses-paid education in a different culture, a different language, a great bunch of people, with a lot of fun and good times. Each September, however, I returned to what I knew was the serious business of my life—being chief scout for the New York Knickerbockers.

Lots of talent was available in the 1964 NBA draft. And those of us involved in making the decisions on the Knicks spent a lot of time in meetings, reviewing films, making phone calls, and getting second and third opinions on players from their coaches or those who had coached against them. We were going back and forth, trying to come up with the right decision.

Jim "Bad News" Barnes out of Texas Western, Lucious Jackson of Pan Am, and Willis Reed of Grambling were the three players we saw as number one draft choice possibilities. We finally decided to go for Barnes in the first round. Philadelphia drafted Jackson. The Boston Celtics picked last in the first round, and when their turn came Willis Reed was still available. I was sure they were going to select him. Instead, they chose Mel Counts, a seven-footer from Oregon State; Red Auerbach claimed he had big plans for Counts as a forward.

Looking back, it seems incredible that Willis lasted to the second round. And when our turn came in the second round we grabbed him.

Willis came from Bernice, Louisiana, and played at Grambling College, not too far from his hometown—which made him a local hero. I spent a lot of time at Grambling then, since it was the premier black college in the United States for athletics. Dr. Ralph W. E. Jones, the president of Grambling, an intelligent and affable man, was also the baseball coach. At basketball games he sat at the end of the floor at court level. Giant Grambling football players were always hovering around him. If fans became unruly, the football players would take care of it, but they didn't have much to do. Crowds there were always pretty orderly.

Many kids who went to white colleges located around Grambling would also attend the games. It was an odd scene. Ten talented black players competing on the basketball court and bunches of white kids in the stands cheering them on. Those days at Grambling foreshadowed what was to come in the NBA, and how the sport would change.

Red Thomas, my Navy buddy, who taught at Northwestern State University, would argue with me about how tall Willis Reed was.

"Hey, I got an idea," Thomas said. "We'll get a tape measure and use it on Willis."

"Are you sure he'll sit still for that?" I asked.

"You can bet on it. Willis is one sweet guy."

Red Thomas approached Willis during a practice one day and told him about our idea.

"Sure. Anything you guys want. Should I take off my sneakers?"

"No, buddy," Thomas told him. "But if we can get you to stand against the wall, it would make it much easier for us."

Willis was a gentle, almost docile guy in those days, always eager to please. Thomas took out the tape measure and held it down on the floor. I strained to raise it to the top of Willis's head.

"Six foot eight, Willis," I said. "You measure six foot eight?"

"If that is what it says, that's what I am."

"But you're listed at six ten?" Thomas was surprised.

"I had nothing to do with that. I guess they did it to make me look taller."

Willis wasn't six ten, but played as if he were. Even though he was crude and raw he was a great shooter for a college player. And I knew that with his weight and strength and his knack of getting position under the basket and keeping others out, Willis would be a great pro center.

With Willis Reed and "Bad News" Barnes, and fine other prospects on the Knicks for the 1964–65 season, there was a lot of optimism in New York. The team got off to a 12–26 start under Eddie Donovan, and Harry Gallatin replaced him as coach. Eddie became general manager. The best Harry could manage was another fourth-place finish for the Knicks. More restlessness among the fans.

Knick coaches were always eager for me to help out with the players on the floor, to help fine-tune their skills. Gallatin was the only coach I didn't work with that way. He had his own way of doing things, especially when it came to strength and conditioning exercises, things that had helped him as a player. As part of his conditioning drill in the 1965–66 training camp in Fairfield, Connecticut, Harry made players carry each other up and down a flight of stairs.

One day Ned Irish visited the camp and almost had a hemorrhage watching in horror as Willis Reed, who at that time was the franchise, huffed and puffed under the load that was "Bad News" Barnes.

Although Irish was livid, he didn't say a word. Right then and there, I knew that Harry Gallatin was on his way out as coach of the New York Knickerbockers.

The team was off to a 6–15 start in the 1965–66 season when Ned Irish replaced Harry Gallatin with Dick McGuire, who had coached at Detroit. I had been a cloak-and-dagger man helping to sneak Dick into a hotel room across from the Garden. Eddie Donovan met with McGuire and made the coaching switch.

Dick McGuire was a quiet, low-keyed man who knew the game of basketball. Not a big disciplinarian, or much on "X's and O's," Dick allowed the guys to play their game and relied a great deal on their pride and professionalism.

Under Dick the Knicks finished fourth that season and the next, and then it became my turn to do it my way.

All the Knick losing years helped make for the winning years that were to be. We were able to sign Bill Bradley, Cazzie Russell, and Walt Frazier as number one picks in the three drafts between 1965 and 1967. We selected Bill Bradley in the last year of the NBA's territorial pick in 1965. After seeing Bill play just once in college I never went out of my way to scout him again, although I saw him play many times after that. He was just great. Bill was scheduled to attend Oxford University after graduation from Princeton but we drafted him anyway.

We took the gamble and waited out the two years while he was at Oxford—and he was worth it.

Cazzie Russell and Dave Bing of Syracuse were the two most highly touted players in the 1966 college draft. We won the coin toss with Detroit for the number one draft, and selected Cazzie. Detroit took Dave. They were both top players, but Cazzie brought a lot of excitement to New York City.

In the 1967 draft Detroit picked first and went for Jimmy Walker of Providence. Baltimore selected second and chose Earl Monroe. Detroit also had the fourth pick, and although Walt Frazier was available, the Pistons already had a standout guard in Walker. So they went for a forward, Sonny Dove of St. John's. We never thought we'd get Walt. It was just a great break that things turned out that way.

There had been frustrations and disappointments along the way, but my vision of building the New York Knickerbockers through the draft was finally beginning to pay off. And the job of pulling the whole thing together was going to be mine. Somehow it was perfect irony that I was going to take over as head coach of the Knicks—a team that my wandering across America had helped create.

I had made more stops than a Greyhound bus driver criss-crossing the United States for nearly a decade as the chief scout of the New York Knickerbockers. All those long rides in rented cars, all those flights to different cities, all those thousands of conversations with coaches and athletic directors, all those lonely meals in roadside diners and tiny restaurants, and all those hours watching games and storing information. I was set to take over as Knick coach, a job I never aimed for, never wanted. Yet everything I had ever done in my basketball life had prepared me for it.

There's a time for everything in a man's life, and this, I knew, was my time, my time to do something special. And I knew I could.

BOOK TWO

CHAPTER 1

I t was December 28, 1967, as I began my first day on the job as coach of the New York Knickerbockers, a team that had finished in fourth place for the past seven seasons. Driving in from my home on Long Island to Madison Square Garden, I thought about the game and how it had changed since I first began playing.

The NBA was being challenged by a new league—the American Basketball Association. George Mikan was the ABA commissioner and several of the guys I had played ball with were coaches: Slater Martin at Houston, Max Zaslofsky at New Jersey, Jim Pollard at Minnesota. And Cliff Hagan, whom I had coached on the St. Louis Hawks, was in charge of the new Dallas team. The ABA played with a red, white, and blue basketball and had a three-point goal for shots made from 25 feet or more. The NBA and the ABA were at war— battling to sign up the best players.

I had changed a lot, too, since I last coached in the NBA with the Hawks. The decade of scouting and talking to 50 or so coaches in a season had given me lots of ideas. I took a little piece here and a little piece there. Winning those three championships in Puerto Rico had given me a lot of confidence. I had developed good work habits and realized my potential as a bench coach and a teacher. I believed the key to winning was the game I was brought up with, team play with an emphasis on hard-nosed defense. I also had an idea of how I was going to run the Knicks, how I would use old-fashioned defense in sort of a new way.

I reviewed in my mind all the players on the Knick roster. As chief scout I had had a hand in selecting eight of the twelve guys: Walt Frazier, Willis Reed, Howard Komives, Emmette Bryant, Dick Van Arsdale, Cazzie Russell, Bill Bradley, and Phil Jackson. I had also scouted Neil Johnson and Nate Bowman, acquired in trades.

Knick trainer Danny Whelan was a guy I knew from my old Rochester days when he was the trainer for the Rochester Red Wings, a top farm team of baseball's St. Louis Cardinals.

I realized as I crossed the Midtown Tunnel into Manhattan that I would be tested by the players. They would try to see if I met their standards. I knew that if I came in and asserted myself right at the start they would realize they would have to meet *my* standards.

But perhaps my greatest asset was the security of knowing I had nothing to lose. I would have rather been a scout anyway! So I decided that the players were going to do things my way, and if they didn't— they wouldn't play.

I always had a thing about being on time. That first day as Knick coach I arrived in the locker room a little early and waited for the team to assemble. Dick Van Arsdale and Howard Komives arrived a couple of minutes late. They had stopped at Nedick's to get a couple of donuts and coffee. It was a perfect opportunity to assert myself. I fined them ten dollars each. It wasn't the money. It was a case of establishing some discipline.

They bitched as if I had fined each of them a billion dollars. They had never experienced anything like that before, being fined for being a couple of minutes late.

"That's my opening shot," I told them. "I mean business, and I want to start school straight."

"This team is going to try to win a championship," I said. "I'm going to work hard as hell and I'm going to make all of you do the same. We're going to have certain rules and those rules will be enforced. For starters, there will be no eating in the locker room before the game and during the halftime."

When I was a scout I winced a lot when I saw Knick players wolfing down locker room "noshes" (snacks). I always felt that was a lousy habit for a player who had to keep in shape. During Dick McGuire's time as coach one of the worst "noshing" offenders was Freddy Crawford. Before halftime Freddy would send the ball boy out to bring him two hot dogs from Nedick's, just outside the old Garden. The ball boy would put the hot dogs in Freddy's locker. During Dick McGuire's halftime talk, Crawford would turn his head to his locker and eat.

One night I was scouting at the Garden and came into the locker room during halftime. After wolfing down his hot dogs, Freddy Crawford turned around to listen to Dick McGuire's halftime talk. All the while Freddy's face was covered with mustard. When McGuire finished his talk, I yelled at Freddy, "Hey, Crawford, what's the matter with your face? It looks like you've got yellow lipstick smeared all over it. Look in the mirror, Freddy!"

He looked at his mustard-decorated face and gave me a sheepish grin.

"Maybe Freddy's modeling some new type of Vaseline," Danny Whelan chipped in.

"Yeah, that's what it is." Freddy smiled, glad for the opportunity to save face. And then he started wiping the mustard off his face. "I guess it don't work too good," Freddy added.

Another thing that definitely didn't work too good was the fact that in the past, Knick coaches had allowed players to bring the wives, the kids, even friends to practice. Sometimes it was pandemonium— players were working out with people cheering, babies crying, radios blaring, cameras snapping.

I cut that nonsense out as soon as I took over as coach. "There will be no more mob scenes at practices," I told them. "You will be working at practices, not having a picnic complete with cheerleaders."

Some of them grumbled. Others just stared at me as if they couldn't believe what they were hearing.

"I know this is a whole new ball game for you," I told them. "No snacks at halftime, no visitors at practice, no bullshit. And practices that will be mostly drill, repetition, and defense. It's going to be hard work for you and for me, but if we win, it'll all be worth it."

From that very first day we practiced 90 minutes a session with none of those minutes wasted. It was one big cram course. At the beginning I had to re-teach them things they had learned, refine their skills. Practices were 90 percent defense. I constantly stressed pressure defense, helping out on defense. I was eager to establish a frame of mind that enabled them to play like a team on offense *and* on defense. Since I wanted to make things automatic in a game—so that all I had to do was call out a number for them to execute a play—I made them work those plays over and over again in practice. It was boring, repetitious grunt work—but they needed it.

"Practice doesn't make perfect," I told them. "Perfect practice does!"

We lost the first two games I coached, 126–115 to Los Angeles and 125–119 to Cincinnati. And lucky for me that management didn't jump too soon. Even though I knew all the abilities of our players from scouting them and watching games from the stands, it's a whole lot different when you're down with them in the trenches.

It's one thing knowing what players can do and another thing making them do it. Coaching on the bench I had to worry about substitutions in the heat of a game. I had to worry about watching the clock and using it properly. I had to worry about proper matchups between our guys and the competition. Manipulation, orchestration, the flow of a game—all of these are a big, big part of bench coaching. And they were all things I never had to worry about before when I was a scout watching games from the stands.

In the third game I coached I recorded my first win, 129–115 over Philadelphia, who had been the previous year's champs. Throughout that game I was constantly jumping off the bench and shouting out directions to our guys.

"Cazzie, be ready. . . . Face the ball, Butch, face the ball . . . Phil . . . be alive out there, know where he is." We played defense from one end of the court to the other, pressing, trapping. I made sure Komives stayed right on top of Wally Jones each time he brought the ball up the court. And Dick Barnett was bellying up and all over Hal Greer even when the Philly guard didn't have the ball. We forced the 76ers into 36 turnovers. Wilt Chamberlain scored 39 points, but our team defense made up for that by limiting the other Philly players.

Dave Zinkoff was Philadelphia's public address announcer for a hundred years. His family owned a delicatessen, and Dave's way of showing he liked you was to give you a salami when you came to Philadelphia.

"Red," he told me in his gravelly voice after the game, "you ain't getting no salami tonight." He was a little upset about our win—the first victory by a Knick team over Philadelphia on their home court since March 1965.

We went on to a record six-game winning streak after the victory over Philadelphia. It was the longest winning streak for a Knick team since 1958–59. The streak wasn't important, but the momentum and the way we played were, because even in our first two losses we showed that we were disrupting clubs with our team defense.

We started to get a feeling of being a team. We played our own style, to our own tempo. The guys began to feel that they were special. They began to develop a sense of pride.

From the start of the season I made a lot of substitutions, playing everybody in a trial-and-error approach, seeking the right combinations for different situations. At times this might have seemed confusing to a lot of people, especially the ballplayers, but I was filing away what I saw, learning who could play defense, who to use in certain pressure spots, what the roles of each of the players on the roster would be. But my object was to quickly get us to the point where each player knew when he was going to play, when he was coming out of a game, what his role was. I knew that would ease their minds.

I made the most use I could of the talents on the roster. Dick Van Arsdale was a hard-working kid. He was strong and could run all night and play defense. Emmette Bryant had quickness and steal value, perfect for my type of team. Walt Bellamy was six eleven and 245 pounds. A big, strong center, he was not as suitable in some ways for the type of team I wanted.

Walt Frazier fit in perfectly. From his defense he was able to get a lot of confidence for his offense. Neil Johnson was a six foot seven New York guy who had played his college ball at Creighton, and he was perfect for special situations. Dick Barnett was very intelligent and could play any kind of basketball you wanted. Howard Komives out of Bowling Green at six one was a hard-nosed, pressing type of player. For Phil Jackson, with his long arms and versatility and intelligence, was ideal for my team. Willis Reed had desire and drive and talent and fit in very well. He was a leader. Nate Bowman was a big backup guy, but he accepted his role. Cazzie Russell was a better player with a team defense that covered up any defensive shortcomings he had. And he could shoot the ball. Dick McGuire had started using Bill Bradley at forward. I completed the conversion. Bill did not have the greatest speed, but our team defense and his intelligence and knowledge of where he had to be on the court more than compensated for that.

After 40 straight days and 40 straight nights of games and practices, I asked Danny Whelan: "Hey, do you think we can take a day off?"

"Are you kidding? I don't know about you, Red," he said, "but I'm exhausted. The players must be dying."

We took a day off, and I went with Danny to the track where we went partners on a two-dollar bet.

I eased up a little bit on the practices—I didn't want to kill the guys, but I still kept up my fines for lateness. It became a game with the players.

"Hey, Coach, he's late," they would yell. "Get him, get him."

"See," I kidded, "it's not me dishing out the fines—it's the guys on the team." After a while players didn't worry about the fines—they learned not to come late because they didn't want the other guys busting their chops.

When I had coached in Ponce I started out wearing wristwatches. But I would get so excited in those games and wave my arms so much that the watch would fly off my wrist. I went through so many wristwatches that I went down to the local *joyeria* (jewelry store), looking for an alternative. I bought a Bullseye pocket watch which cost three bucks and had a big white face and black numbers. I loved that ticker.

The players on the Knicks had watches that cost five thousand, ten thousand dollars. Those watches were encrusted with jewels and loaded with all kinds of gadgets.

"Hey, Red," they would kid me. "Your watch is an old piece of crap. The time is all wrong. Why don't you dump it and get something modern?"

"I don't give a damn how much your watch cost or how modern it is," I would tell them. "This Bullseye is the official timekeeper and if it says you're late—you're late!"

Over the years that old Bullseye watch helped me collect about five thousand dollars in fine money. When did you last hear of a three-dollar investment that earned that much money?

We were also starting to bring in a lot of money for the Knicks as attendance kept getting better and better. Fans came to the Garden to watch us blow other teams away by 15, 20 points. Word started getting around that we were no fluke. Our record was based on hard work and catching the other teams with something relatively new—team defense. Opposing teams weren't too happy being picked up and pressed. That took players out of their regular pattern and brought the talent differential closer between teams.

When we first started doing it nobody paid much attention. I never talked too much about what we were doing and how we were doing it. I almost killed a couple of players when they started explaining our methods. I didn't want to give away any trade secrets. Now I guess I can.

Having studied what was taking place in the NBA at that time, I realized it was basically an offensively oriented league. Most of the teams won their games by scoring points quickly and in bunches. The Celtics stressed defense, but their type of defense was built around Bill Russell, not on a total team concept. Ours was set up to be a trapping, pressing, five-man approach.

Everybody had always said that it was impractical to press full court, to have defensive players double-team the guy with the ball to try to gain control of it, to trap at every opportunity. Teams generally used those defensive techniques when they fell behind in a game. I thought that if the technique was effective in helping teams come back in the late stages of a game, why not use it early in a game, and sometimes throughout an entire game?

I realized that using that technique would eliminate the surprise aspects of the trap and the full court press; nevertheless, I knew that kind of defense, if used properly, accomplishes a great deal. It gives the other team less time to use the 24-second clock because they're fighting like hell to get the ball over the midcourt line. Additionally, most of the things that they have planned in set plays go out the window. An opposing team's formal offense suddenly becomes almost useless for them. They wind up with less time to pass the ball and with less time to take their shots.

I knew that my players had the ability to do almost anything I asked them to do. My concept of all-out team defense was very, very hard work for our players. I realized, however, that the guards were essentially the only ones who pressed and that when they got tired I could put someone else in to give them a blow.

Although all the players on the team were hungry and eager to succeed, it was a bitch of a selling job at the start to convince them to do it my way. I had to stay on their tails.

"One day you'll all be getting credit for steals and praise for your defensive ability," I told them.

The rap on some of our players before I took over was that they were not good at defense. There's no player that is truly a good defensive player one-on-one against a great offensive player. It's almost impossible for one defender to consistently stop a great shooter once he gets to his spot or is able to pick up a screen, a block from a guy on his team. I always realized this and made our guys realize it. And with our team approach they all became better defensive players.

When we pressed and trapped as a team, we did a lot of things off the traps that pushed the opposition from their strengths into their weaknesses. The pressure forced them into one-on-one shooting situations. With the clock running, all of that pressure worked in our favor. Our players were poised to capitalize on any mistakes, to steal the ball, to make the other team force a shot, to make them make one more move, one more pass. We and the clock became the enemy for the other team. And if the game was at the Garden with the crowd going with us, the other team was in deep trouble. In a sense our defense created a great deal of our offense.

I totally overhauled the Knick offense with an emphasis on

discipline. We used a set offense with very little free-lancing to make sure the guys would pass the ball a lot and be in proper positions to receive the ball when it was passed to them. I borrowed something from football by using offensive formations—structured kinds of setups. Off each formation we ran our plays. With repetition everyone on our team automatically knew where the next pass was going.

"See the ball! See the ball!" I must have screamed out those words thousands of times. The guys on the Knicks must have heard those words in their sleep. It was my way of making them aware of where the basketball was on the court, what the passing lanes were like for offense and defense, what the flow of the game was.

Holzman's law on offense became "Hit the open man!" It was a two-way street—guys had to get open for a good percentage shot and the passer had to hit that player with a good pass. When we did it properly, it was a thing of beauty: Bradley passing the ball to Frazier, then quickly cutting to the basket and Walt hitting him with the ball . . . Willis in the pivot flicking a pass to Barnett cutting down the lane for a lay-up . . . Frazier pulling up at the foul line for a jumper, faking the shot and passing off to Reed. . . . The combinations were endless. With those intelligent players and ball movement and unselfish team play we whipped the ball and we whipped the other team.

A set pre-game routine for me and the players on the Knicks became a way of life. That cut down any misunderstandings and kept surprises to a minimum. There was enough excitement to handle during the games. All the players were expected to be in the locker room an hour and a half before game time. I always had a film of the team we were opposing that night running without sound. It was a good device to refresh our players' memories. It was optional for our guys to look at as they were dressing and getting ready for the game.

I looked at the film during the day of a game but seldom made the players come in during the afternoon to watch it with me, not wanting to disturb their rest. If they saw something on the film they wanted to talk about, I was always available to get into it with them.

When our team went out for warmups before a game, I remained behind in my office or the locker room. I always hated waiting for the game to start, and pacing was part of my way of loosening up. I must have done thousands of miles of road work in those locker rooms. I wouldn't come out onto the floor until a couple of minutes before game time because I found that if I was out there too early, I became too accessible to people. They meant well, but they all wanted to talk. You don't feel like talking just before a game—you're too busy concentrating.

Willis Reed was the captain of the Knicks, and he was the boss out there during warmups. A gem of a guy to have on your team because of the example he set, Willis worked hard even in the warmups. Whenever we had a rookie we would pair him up with Willis. They were lucky because Willis always went first class. He was very good-natured and would always take care of them. He would also take charge of them.

"Hey, rookie," he'd shout. "Carry those bags. That's what rookies are supposed to do." They would jump to it.

Sometimes a rookie would need money and Willis would peel off three hundred or a thousand dollars. Then he would hold the guy gently by the lapels.

"We get thirteen checks," he'd say with a smile on his face. "When the last check is due, I'll remind you about it a day before. When you get paid, I want the money you owe me right in my hand or that will be the end of you! You understand?" They always paid right on time.

Toughness characterized Willis. He had an incredible ability to tolerate pain. Willis had his nose broken in a few games, and each time it happened he returned to the bench and told Danny to pop his nose back in. And then he went out again to play.

Willis could always play hurt. In a game against San Francisco players were bumping each other around, and it was fierce out there on the floor. Suddenly, in a skirmish under the basket, a hand came out of nowhere and slammed into Rick Barry's mouth. The way Barry bitched it was as if he had parted with all the teeth in his mouth. Actually he had parted with just one tooth, and play was stopped while guys crawled around on their hands and knees, trying to locate the missing tooth.

Barry complained that Walt Bellamy was responsible for the dental damage. We all knew it couldn't have been "Bells"—he was a conscientious objector.

During halftime Willis matter-of-factly went over to Danny Whelan. "Is there anything you can do about this knuckle of mine, Danny?"

Danny and I took a look at Willis's knuckle. "I think you need a dentist, not a trainer," Danny said, giving Willis that big grin. Embedded in Willis's knuckle was Rick Barry's missing tooth. Willis had played almost the entire first half with it there.

After the game was over, it was over. I never closed my door to the press, win, lose, or draw—for more than a minute or so. I would tell the team about the next day's schedule—when, where, and how we were going. And then I would talk to the press for as long as they wanted.

Reporters were sometimes stunned by the answers I gave them. At times we might play better in the second half of a game than we had in the first half.

"Coach, what did you do that was so different in the second half?"

"We did the same things," I would respond, "but we executed just a little better. I don't know. What do you guys think?"

It wasn't a satisfying answer for them, and some reporters thought I was being evasive. Actually, it was an honest answer. Sometimes in the second half a small adjustment changed a game around. You used the first half as a guideline for the rest of a game. For example, if you used play B in the first half and it didn't work because a player coming off a screen had not set his man up properly, you would then run the same thing again only making sure that the man worked harder and more efficiently to come off the screen.

Halftime was reserved for assessing, evaluating, fine-tuning. I always asked for opinions and suggestions from the players, and if a guy suggested something and I agreed to use it—I knew they would all break their butts to make that suggestion work. I never, however, used a play in a game that we hadn't practiced before.

The press attention on me kept increasing. This was kind of tough on a guy who valued his privacy, preferred to stay in the background, do his coaching, and let the players grab the headlines. A few writers called me a tough interview. They were always looking for an angle, for something to write about the Knicks and me. I gave them a lot of time but some of them thought they didn't get enough quotes. One writer characterized me as "cagey."

There was always a lot of good-natured kidding between the media and me. And some of the things they thought were funny made their way into the newspapers.

"Red, William Holzman is your legal name," a reporter began. "How come you don't have a middle initial?"

"When I was born my parents were too poor to afford a middle initial for me." When that answer appeared in the newspaper, I realized they were getting desperate.

The Garden crowd consisted of a lot of classy dressers. Some of our own players also went in for clothes in a big way. I dressed conservatively.

"Red, you dress like it was 1956," a reporter started in with me, "and yet you're coaching a team located in the heart of the garment center, where all the latest fashions and styles are introduced. Why is that?"

"I figure I'm going to work," I told the writer. "And the way to dress is conservatively. I have nine suits, all Brooks Brothers, all ordered by phone, all the same style and color. It's simpler that way." That answer also made its way into the newspapers. Those guys *really* needed quotes.

Some of the reporters couldn't get over how calm I was. Most of the time I really was calm because I realized basketball is a game in which the outcome depends so much at times on two guys—the refs—who aren't even playing. It could be frustrating, but I learned to accept things—especially that final is final. I would never downgrade another team or another player or chew out any of my players in public. I also didn't believe in second-guessing myself or others. I might moan a little after a loss, especially a tough loss, but I didn't go into hysterics the way some coaches did.

The press seemed surprised that I was able to put even a resounding defeat behind me quickly and start planning for the next game.

"How do you manage to do that?" a reporter popped the question.

"Because I realize that the only real catastrophe is coming home and finding out that there's no more scotch left in the house." That one-liner made the newspapers too.

Free advice was also always part of the scene. Letters would come from all over telling me to "put this guy in more, take that guy out." I had suggestions for a five-guard offense, for playing with three guys, for Willis to bring the ball up the court to draw fouls. I answered every one of the letters I ever received, unless it was of the sick variety, since I never wanted to encourage those kinds of people. There were also a few threatening letters and on some nights we had to have extra security people on hand. Thankfully there was not too much of that.

The only thing I went out of my way to avoid was to become adopted by someone as a pen pal. One guy kept writing to me from Mexico. I answered him a couple of times, but he kept right on writing and I realized he was becoming a pen pal and never wrote to him again. The guy always wrote the same letter.

Please send me your photo with your authentic autograph (*not printed*) please. And send me your authentic autograph in this card. Please, please, answer me. I write you a lot of times. Be kind for this only time. My admiration for you deserves your attention. I'm poor and I not have enough money for write you. ANSWER ME. Sorry but I do not have envelope with stamps of your country for remit the photo. PLEASE, PLEASE answer ME. I write you too much. I'm exhausted. (is fun). Thank you very much and forgive my rudeness. From Mexico with love for you.

One of the perils of coaching an NBA team is the constant travel all over the country in all kinds of weather. Once we were flying through the Midwest and the plane started shaking. We were caught in the middle of a blizzard. We landed in Chicago and managed to get accommodations in a small hotel. Since there weren't many rooms available, we all had to double and triple up.

I doubled Nate Bowman up with sportswriter Augi Borgi. Both of them were free spirits and I figured they'd make a good team. Everyone was dead tired from the bumping around we took except for Nate who was always exuberant.

While the rest of us went to our rooms to sack out, Nate spent some time in the hotel lobby with a parrot he spotted in a cage. He would always do unusual things like that, so I didn't pay much attention. I was coming down in the elevator the next morning for breakfast, when Bowman and Borgi came into the elevator.

"How'd you guys sleep?" I asked.

"Not bad, Red," Borgi said, "except that Nate mumbled in his sleep all night about a parrot."

"Yeah," Nate interrupted Borgi. "And you gave me the creeps, sleeping with one eye open."

We stepped off the elevator and into the lobby and noticed a big commotion around the parrot's cage. The bird kept chanting "Mother f-----, mother f-----!" Guests were furious. Some of them were checking out of the hotel.

Nate Bowman, like a six-foot-ten peacock, turned to me with a great big grin on his face. "Red, you know that parrot was one of the quickest learners I ever had the pleasure to work with."

An interesting sidelight to that 1967–68 season was the nostalgia of coaching the Knicks in the last game played at the old Madison Square Garden and all the excitement of coaching them in the first game played at the new Garden.

The last game at the old Garden was played before a sellout crowd of 18,499 on February 10, 1968. An exhibition game between the East Coast Rens and the Fabulous Magicians with Marcus Haynes preceded our game.

Marcus Haynes, who would have been a star in straight basketball, put on a show. He was about five ten and slender but very strong. He slithered about with the ball, dribbled while on his back or his stomach, dribbled the ball between his legs and through all five guys on the opposition and gave his teammates a chance to get a breather. The fans got a real kick out of him and so did I and the guys on the Knicks.

"That Marcus Haynes is great, Red," Walt Frazier said. "Maybe we should try to sign him up."

"It's not a bad idea, Walt, but I think Marcus is happy doing what he's doing. Besides, we have you."

In the main event that night we beat Philadelphia 115–97. Walt

Frazier, who was just three years old when the original Knicks began in the Garden, put on a show. Walt scored 23 points, had 15 assists, and grabbed 15 rebounds.

"What were you doing, Walt, trying to upstage Haynes?"

"No, Red. Maybe Haynes just gave me some inspiration. And since it was the last game at the Garden, maybe I'll be remembered for what I did tonight."

"Walt," I told him, "you'll be remembered for much more than that."

The game was also a reunion of sorts. Philadelphia's coach, Alex Hannum, my former player, teammate, and successor with the St. Louis Hawks and I were hit with technicals. The ref who dished out the damage was my old City College teammate, Norm Drucker, who always bent over backward to be fair.

The new Madison Square Garden was opened up on February 14, 1968, with a lot of hype and hoopla, and deep down I felt good about the whole thing. The old Garden represented the tradition of the past. The new Garden represented the future of a team I believed could keep on winning.

We defeated San Diego 114–102 in the second game of a doubleheader to get off to a good start in the new Garden. That night was also witness to an interesting irony. The first basket scored in the new Garden was by an impressive player on the Detroit Pistons. His name was Dave DeBusschere.

John Condon was on the scene with the Knicks even then as the public address announcer. Some P.A. guys used the mike to rile up the home crowd, but John never did. He's always been one of the fairest announcers in the NBA.

The brand new microphone that John used that night had a few bugs, and John struggled quite a bit with it throughout his announcements. There was relief in his voice when he finally announced: "Two minutes left."

"In the game or in the mike?" yelled Dick Barnett.

"In you, Dick," screamed a fan.

Despite the small problems, moving out of the old Garden, which was kind of rundown, to a brand new place made everyone connected with the Knicks very happy.

The vision of Irving Mitchell Felt, and his family in the real estate business, was the inspiration for Madison Square Garden Center. Felt made people comfortable, and he always took good care of me. I also became friends with Alvin Cooperman and Manny Azenberg, who worked under Felt, handling entertainment at the Garden. They both went on to become famous Broadway producers.

Teaching all I had learned about the game to young players on the Knicks was a big part of my work at the start. That first season I spent a lot of time with Bill Bradley and Walt Frazier, both rookies.

Brought up in Crystal City, Missouri, Bill Bradley was an incredible high school basketball player. He could have probably gone to any college in America on a basketball scholarship. But he chose Princeton University, and paid his own way because Ivy League schools did not award athletic scholarships.

Princeton's basketball team won three Ivy League titles while Bill was there. A three-time all-American, Bill averaged 30.1 points a game. In 1964 Bill was the only junior on the U.S. basketball team that won the gold medal at the Tokyo Olympics. He finished his collegiate career as the fourth leading scorer in college basketball history.

Bill Bradley's greatest college game was on December 30, 1964, at Madison Square Garden in the semifinals of the Holiday Festival. His Princeton team was up by eight points over Michigan, which had Cazzie Russell and was then the top team in the country. Bill had scored 41 of Princeton's 75 points—even though guys were hanging all over him. With 4:37 left in the game, Bill fouled out and was given one of the longest standing ovations in Garden history. With Bill out of the game, Michigan rallied to win by two points.

When Bill graduated from Princeton he accepted a Rhodes scholarship to Oxford University in England. Even though I knew this meant we would have to wait two years for him, I didn't hesitate to recommend we make him our number one draft choice.

His four-year contract with the Knicks was for an estimated $500,000. "I just wanted to see how I could do against the best players in the world," Bradley said after signing for what was a ton of money then. "I just had to know."

When Bradley first joined the Knicks, guys kidded him about the big money he was earning. Howard Komives nicknamed him "Dollar Bill." Other players called him "Superman," and asked Bill when he was going into the phone booth for his quick change.

Bill could be funny by design but he was never an oddball, even though his tastes and interests were far different from the other players. He liked museums, shows, books, and his friends were intellectual, busy guys.

Yet, with all of this, Bill was always one of the guys on the team, always wanting to keep his low profile image. He wore clothes that looked like hand-me-downs—but that, too, was part of his way.

One of Bill's favorite garments was an old tan raincoat, so old and in such bad shape that it looked almost black. Donnie May was one of the most meticulous players I ever coached, and one night he was sitting down to get suited up for a game. Bill Bradley came into the locker room and took off his old blackened raincoat and laid it down near Donnie.

"Ugh, ugh!" was Donnie's reaction when he caught sight of the raincoat. He picked it up and heaved it to the other end of the locker room.

Bill never even noticed. His head was buried in a big book as he took advantage of a few spare minutes before the game.

Later on Bill's wardrobe improved dramatically as the result of a deal he made with Dick Barnett. Dick would help pick out Bill's clothes and Bill would help Dick with his studies when he went back to school.

Even then Bill was intensely interested in politics and arranged many appointments and meetings on community matters. Danny Whelan and I made a deal with him. We collected chits whenever Bill wanted some time off to keep an appointment and made Bill promise that when he became president of the United States he would give us good jobs. I've still got those IOUs around the house somewhere. . . .

Bradley needed confidence to learn the pro game. I realized that playing him at forward would help his game by keeping him away from getting beaten by quick guards. I taught him positioning on defense and how to avoid turning his head when he was guarding a player. Bill also had a tendency to reach in on defense to try to get the ball. His body would get thrown off balance. I made him stop doing that and showed him how to get his body into the right position for defense.

I spent a lot of time talking with Bill and demonstrating how he could get free for his best shot. With his natural touch Bill almost never needed to force a shot. Bill had great intelligence and was also such a perfectionist that he picked up all my tips very quickly.

He was one of the hardest workers I ever coached. Working hard was his way of life. He worked hard when he went to museums. He worked hard when he read books—he was always reading two or three books at a time. He worked hard at basketball. Bill was a basketball junkie—he loved the game, and he just loved to play all the time.

Although he came out of the Ivy League and a cushier background than a lot of the players in the NBA, Bill was as tough as they come. On defense he was an irritating player. He'd push a little, stick his hands all over a guy he was guarding, do anything he could to throw an opponent off his stride. Sometimes Bill came back to the bench after a skirmish, with his body looking like it had been flicked with a razor—there were cuts and scrapes all over him. His classic battles were with tough-scoring forwards like Jack Marin, John Havlicek, and Rick Barry. Those guys would get annoyed at the way Bill hounded them on defense. Whenever they matched up with Bill there would be lots of pushing and shoving. It was funny, because none of them could fight their way out of a paper bag. Most basketball players can't.

Bill Bradley had a tremendous ability to play with pain and discomfort. If some of the players I coached got a tiny cut on their finger, they'd bitch as if they had gotten smacked with an ax. Bill went the other way—he came to play.

Once in San Diego we had a lot of players either sick or hurt. In the locker room Bill looked green and feverish. He threw up a couple of times.

"Maybe you should go back to the hotel and sleep it off," I advised Bill.

"No, Red, I'll be all right. You can start me."

"Are you sure, Bill?"

"Sure. It's just a little virus."

The game got under way and Bill played. Kids usually work hard wiping up the sweat off the floor from the players. In that game they were swabbing what Bill kept dropping.

Bill vomited about six times on the court. "Whoosh, whoosh," players were ducking to get out of the way. He was sick but he was playing great.

During our first time-out I tried to take him out of the game. "The team needs me, Red," Bradley protested. "Besides, I'm really not feeling that bad."

In fact it got so bad that I hesitated to call time-outs because each time he came back to the huddle he vomited. The stuff got on my shoes, on Danny Whelan's sneakers.

Bill played great that game, and although we were short in manpower his extra effort made up for it, enabling us to win. Bill Bradley played all out when it mattered, and when it didn't matter at all. He was always ready.

Bill studied the game, and his knowledge of it was as good as anybody's. He believed in team basketball and made up for his lack of speed and physical ability with his knowledge of the game and ability to be in the right place at the right time. He made sure he was always in great shape so he could keep running and moving all the time.

There's been so much said and written about Bill Bradley, but I can sum up my own feelings briefly: He was the kind of guy every father would want as a son and every basketball coach would want as a player.

When I scouted Walt Frazier at Southern Illinois University I knew he would be a fine guard in the pros because of his strength, quickness, and defensive ability.

When I replaced Dick McGuire as coach and switched the emphasis of the Knicks to defense, Walt fit in perfectly because that was his game. He was able to use his speed, his size, his strong hands. And through tough defense, Walt was able to create a lot of opportunities for his offense—scoring off steals, breakaways, and busted plays.

I spent a lot of time with Walt, and as we worked together I saw him become the forerunner of what is today called a point guard. I taught him to cut down on his dribble, to pass or hold the ball depending on the situation. Penetration also became a big part of

Walt's game—and I showed him how to move in close off the foul line and either drive for a basket or pull up for a short jumper.

Under my system Walt Frazier functioned like a scrambling quarterback. He could run with the ball, dribble it, pass the ball off to a guy in the "end zone," or take his shot. Walt was so strong that he could take and make a shot even if he got hit or a couple of guys were hanging all over him.

We also worked with Walt to discipline him to shoot from medium range, because his deep shot was not that effective, and he ultimately developed his medium range shot into a deadly weapon.

Having a guy with Walt's hands and quickness on the team, I was able to innovate in ways that helped us win a lot of games. We double-teamed to steal the ball. We'd force a player into a pocket between two of our players in the middle or the sideline and try to create a blind side. We knew that if we put enough pressure on that player, he would assume there was an unguarded player on his team. He would throw the ball to the unguarded player. A third man on the Knicks, a forward or center, would cheat to get into position to make the steal from the uncovered man. I drilled that play into the practice over and over so that it became instinctive.

Walt had a great deal of pride and loved to be in the spotlight. His coolness and kind of effortless play made him one of the most popular players ever to perform for the Knicks. The movie *Bonnie and Clyde* was big at that time and Danny Whelan gave Walt the nickname Clyde. It caught on with the media, and the fans and Walt enjoyed that. He became a dapper dresser, a guy with a mink coat, a Rolls Royce, a fancy beard, and there was all that publicity about how all kinds of women were attracted to him.

Some people made a thing about all of that, but it was all for show. Although Walt's image went through a big change, his personality stayed the same. Through all the years I coached him, Walt was a laid-back, quiet, nice man who enjoyed playing basketball. He was very vain about his body and always took good care of it, which meant doing things in moderation. A very stable personality, Walt was always ready to play and gave 100 percent all the time.

Neither Bradley nor Frazier won the Rookie of the Year award in 1967–68. It went to Baltimore's Earl Monroe, who won it on merit, averaging nearly 25 points a game. The "Pearl" finished fourth in NBA scoring average behind Wilt Chamberlain, Elgin Baylor, and Dave Bing. Chamberlain won his third straight Most Valuable Player award.

It was a very good year for those players. It was also a very good year for the New York Knickerbockers. In my first year as coach the team played 28–17 basketball. That figured out to a .636 percentage compared to .604 for the same period for the Boston Celtics. And the Celts won the NBA championship that season.

The Knicks drew more than a half million in home attendance for the first time in their history. We wound up in third place—the best finish by a Knick team since 1958–59. And we won more games than any other Knick team since 1953–54.

Not only my defensive philosophy, but my team offense concept was taking hold. Willis Reed, Dick Barnett, Walt Bellamy, Dick Van Arsdale, and Cazzie Russell all averaged in double figures in scoring. And Komives, Bradley, Jackson, and Frazier collectively averaged better than 30 points a game. In the playoffs, we were matched against Philadelphia. It was a team with a lot of firepower with Wilt Chamberlain, Billy Cunningham, Chet Walker, and Hal Greer. We lost the first game, 118–110. Cazzie Russell was an offensive machine in the second game, playing before 19,500 at Madison Square Garden. He paced our 128–117 win. The score didn't truly reflect what happened, as the 76ers kept coming up with rallies late in the game before we finally put them away.

Game three, played at the Palestra because the roof of the Spectrum in Philadelphia had been damaged by high winds, was a wild one. We were behind by 14 at one stage, then by ten points late in the fourth quarter. Cazzie's basket with 26 seconds left in the game gave him 40 points in the game and gave us a 113–111 lead. We fouled Wilt a couple of times and he missed five straight free throws, but Chet Walker got free and put in a shot that sent the game into OT.

Both teams scrambled through that overtime. It was frantic. Billy Cunningham was lost to Philly on the first play when he dove for the ball and suffered a fractured forearm. I know that just made them play harder. We wound up losing the game by one point.

We played harder and held them under 100 points to win the

fourth game in New York, 107–98. However, we lost Walt Frazier when he injured his leg in the first half. Without Walt we were weakened defensively. Philadelphia took the next two games and knocked us out of the playoffs. The 76ers then went on to take the Celtics all the way to the seventh game of the Eastern Division finals before being eliminated themselves.

The fans in New York City were hungry for a winning basketball team, and what we had done created a lot of excitement. It was a great year for the Knicks and any management thoughts of my being an interim coach were dropped. Pressure was put on me to stay on. Although I would have been happy to go back to scouting, I agreed to continue as coach—not continuing would have been a mistake for me and the team.

Sometimes when a new coach comes in and takes over a basketball team there's a change. That's the way it had worked out for us, but now the big challenge was to see if we could sustain it.

CHAPTER 2

My old St. Louis Hawks team moved to Atlanta for the 1968–69 season. Two new teams, the Phoenix Suns and Milwaukee Bucks, entered the league, bringing the total number of franchises to 14.

In the expansion draft held to stock the new franchises with players, we lost Dick Van Arsdale to Phoenix and Emmette Bryant to Milwaukee.

We hated to lose those two players. They were intelligent and played good defense. Yet we had to lose somebody. We could have placed Howard Komives on the expansion list, but we knew he was more marketable than Van Arsdale or Bryant, and as it turned out later we were right.

We picked tenth in the regular draft and chose Bill Hosket, who had played well at Ohio State. That year the only real quality players were Elvin Hayes, selected first by San Diego, and Wes Unseld, picked second by Baltimore. Considering what was available to us, Hosket wasn't a bad choice. He knew what his role would be and that he wouldn't play that much because there were better players ahead of him. As it turned out, Bill's effectiveness was limited by problems he had with his knees. He also had to struggle keeping his weight down. Donnie May out of Dayton University also made the club.

In training camp I continued to work the guys hard. I thought we had the talent and potential to improve our record, but it looked like Boston and Philadelphia would be outstanding teams in our Eastern Division and that we would fall in a little behind them.

In the Western Division, Atlanta, San Francisco, and Los Angeles shaped up as the best teams. The Lakers had acquired Wilt Chamberlain and given him a huge contract to bring him to a team that already included Elgin Baylor and Jerry West.

Our season got off to a disappointing start considering what we had accomplished the year before. We lost six of our first 19 games. And there were some who thought what I had done with the Knicks the previous season was just a fluke. I didn't get rattled and neither did management. We were able to turn things around pretty quickly by winning 12 of our next 16 games.

And then on December 19, 1968, just about a week before my first anniversary as coach, we completed what proved to be the best trade in the history of the New York Knickerbockers, acquiring Dave DeBusschere from Detroit. I had scouted Dave when he was in college and always thought he was a terrific player, but Detroit had been able to select him as a territorial choice. A 1962 graduate of the University of Detroit, Dave was a great all-around athlete. During the early 1960s he was a pitcher with the Chicago White Sox. He played for the Pistons for six and a half years—two and a half of them as a player-coach.

Eddie Donovan and I spent months going back and forth with the Pistons to make the deal. It was finally completed when we agreed to add Howie Komives in the trade along with Walt Bellamy. I would have even given more.

I never had any worries about that trade because I knew Dave would be the final piece of the whole I was building.

Dave was only six six, but weighed about 235. A big burly guy, strong as a bull, a blue-collar basketball player, Dave would get out there and bang it out. He was very intelligent, wasn't hungry about his points, and helped young players.

When we traded for him, we believed DeBusschere was a great player. Dave turned out to be even better than we thought. All too often a player comes to a team in a deal and you find there are problems: he's got bad hands, poor training habits, stuff you never noticed before coaching or playing against him. Dave had no problems. All the players respected him for his ability and leadership qualities. Dave was smart enough to realize that playing unselfishly was in his best interests and would make him a better basketball player. For all-around play, I rank him as one of the best all-time forwards.

After the trade, the roles of the players on the Knicks became more defined. With Bellamy gone, Willis Reed had the center position all to himself, with backup help from Nate Bowman. With Komives gone, Walt Frazier moved up from the third guard to start along with Dick Barnett.

In 1965–66 I had recommended the trade that brought Barnett to the Knicks from Los Angeles for Bob Boozer. Because Dick was kind of flamboyant, people never gave him the credit he deserved for being an all-around basketball player. In my book he ranks as one of the all-time great guards in the NBA.

I knew Dick from my days of scouting him at Tennessee State, at that time a black college. Syracuse selected him in the 1959 draft, before we had a chance. Left-handed all the way, with a great touch and fine form, Dick's minutes increased when I became coach of the Knicks. He loved to play basketball and had a lot of pride. He knew when he was going to play, and how he was going to play. His intelligence and great ability always kept him in the game.

Teaming Barnett with Frazier was just perfect. Dick was a great off guard and a fine complement for a guy handling the ball. Able to move very well without the ball and get the pass, Dick knew how to set up his man for the screen and get open for his shot. One of Dick's favorite expressions was "Fall back, baby!" Whenever he took his left-handed jump shot, that was his way of telling the other Knicks that his shot was going in and they should fall back on defense.

People didn't realize that Dick Barnett was a hell of a defensive player and could perform in a free-lance atmosphere or a set style. Very often he took on the tough guards on the other teams and had to get physical with them. At six four and 190, Dick could belly-up pretty good.

* * *

Part of our locker room scene was Walt Frazier coming in wearing a black and white belted leather coat and an Al Capone suit, followed by Dick Barnett in his Carnaby Street creations. Dick would lay down his cane, take off his cape, his homburg, his spats—he was one of the sharpest dressers in the business. Then he would go into a monologue on his old neighborhood, the latest news, the meaning of life and death.

Guys would come to the locker room early simply to listen to Barnett. Some of the guys might have seemed to just be tying their shoelaces, but they all listened. Dick had the gift of gab. He always had something going for him. One of his pastimes was postcard chess. He'd play many games at the same time with different players in the NBA by marking his chess moves on postcards and mailing them out. He'd get very excited about strategy, and sometimes impatient when he didn't get a quick enough response from one of the other players.

With Barnett and Frazier as the starting backcourt, Mike Riordan became the third guard. A supplementary pick after ten rounds in the 1967 draft, Mike had played in the shadow of Jimmy Walker at Providence College. A tough, strong New York City kid, Mike would take a hard workout before a game and then shower and be ready. Others following that routine might have left their game on the floor.

At that time in the NBA you could give up one point to try to get two by fouling a guy and then getting possession of the ball after he took a foul shot. My innovation was to have Mike come into the game just to give a foul and then sit down on the bench. It was a tactic I used to keep the starting guards out of foul trouble. Mike eventually made himself a great player, but at the start he understood his role and he did it gladly to survive. He was good at it. He went out there and he nailed them.

That 1968–69 season Cazzie Russell played in just 50 games and Phil Jackson in only 47. They were both sidelined the last two months of the season with injuries, but we still managed a 54–28 record, at that time the most wins of any Knick team in history. We set a club record for the most consecutive wins with 11. We had the fourth best offensive record in the NBA. Seven of our players had scoring averages in double figures. And defensively we gave up just 105.2 points a game to lead the league in that category.

We finished in third place, only a game behind Philadelphia, and three games behind first-place Baltimore. Boston wound up in fourth place in the Eastern Division with their worst record in thirteen years. The Lakers won the Western Division title with a 55–27 record.

The Bullets were our competition in the opening round of the playoffs. Leaping from last place the year before to a first-place finish, they had Wes Unseld, the first guy to win both the Rookie of the Year award and Most Valuable Player award since Wilt Chamberlain in 1960. Earl Monroe and Kevin Loughery, who averaged almost 49 points between them, complemented Unseld's pivot play very well.

The Baltimore guys made a mistake—or somebody misquoted them—but it came out in the newspapers that they would rather play us in the first round of the playoffs than anybody else. Our players were not too happy about that. Walt Frazier made up the slogan: "They Chose Us!" And the media built the whole thing up into a grudge match.

We swept Baltimore in four games, winning the Eastern Division semifinals and becoming the first Knick team to move past the first round in sixteen years.

The defending NBA champs, the Boston Celtics, were our competition in the Eastern Division finals. We had beaten them six out of seven games during the regular season. And the press made a big deal out of the fact that the Celtics were an old team and that we had the home court edge.

The first game was played on Sunday afternoon April 6, 1969, before a sellout crowd at Madison Square Garden and a national television audience. Our guys didn't play as well as they could have, and at one point we were losing by 25 points.

We came back but not far enough. The Celtics took that first game 108–100.

They got off to a 25–9 roll in the second game in Boston and beat us 112–97. We won the third game in New York 101–91. I knew that if we won game four in Boston we'd get back the home court edge and it would be a two-out-of-three-game series with two of those games in New York.

There were 15 ties in that fourth game. With less than 24 seconds left in the game, we were trailing by one point. Frazier had the ball, and the Celtics swarmed all over him. He passed off to Willis who took a shot and missed. We lost 97–96.

We beat Boston 112–104 in game five at Madison Square Garden. Game six was scheduled on their home court, and we knew if we won it the edge would swing back to us, because the seventh game was scheduled for Madison Square Garden.

Walt Frazier played in that sixth game on a bad leg. That hurt us. Willis tried to take up the slack. He scored 32 points. We came close— as close as you can get—and we lost the game by one point, 106–105. Boston went on to defeat the Lakers for the NBA title for their eleventh championship in thirteen years. That was the final season of Sam Jones and Bill Russell, who had meant so much to the Celtics.

One thing that has always been part of the NBA is the constant change. In addition to Sam Jones and Bill Russell, two other fine players, Wayne Embry and Rudy Larusso, also retired that year. It was also the first season that Bill Russell and Wilt Chamberlain did not make the All-Star team. They were replaced by Wes Unseld and Willis Reed. And San Diego, not an especially good team, was pushed into the playoffs by a rookie named Elvin Hayes who led the league in scoring.

For the Knicks things kept on changing for the better. Even financially things were looking up. We set an NBA attendance record, drawing 569,163 in 37 regular season home dates. There were also 14 sellouts at the Garden, including seven in a row and five-for-five in the playoffs against the Bullets and Celtics.

Years before, people had stood on the corner trying to give away Knick tickets. Now fans were all over me and the players trying to get tickets. That 1968–69 season we became the first team in the history of the National Basketball Association to play before a million fans. The Celtics had all those banners hanging in the Boston Garden, but they never had done that. Something the Knicks had never done was win an NBA championship, and I looked forward to 1969–70, knowing that we had a chance. I realized that we had to go through the entire year without a lot of injuries to key people, that there were a lot of tough teams in the NBA, that we would have to sustain our drive through a very long season, that everything would have to fall into place. But still, we had a chance.

John Warren out of St. John's was our number one pick in the 1969 draft as we selected eleventh out of 14 teams. Boston picked Jo Jo White just before us. I had seen White play in the Pan Am games and there was no question that I wanted him. But Jo Jo was another player that we just got aced out of. In that draft Milwaukee won a coin toss with Phoenix and selected Lew Alcindor. Phoenix wound up with Neal Walk.

The 1969–70 season marked the return to the Knicks of Dave Stallworth, our second pick in the 1965 draft. Dave had been away for a couple of years after having suffered a heart attack. I was a little protective of him in training camp and when the season began, but he said he was all right, and the doctors gave him a clean bill of health.

I had scouted Dave at Wichita State and always liked him. He had a mean "game face" when he played, but actually he was one of the nicest guys I ever coached. Dave became one of my favorite players. He had a great attitude, terrific speed, fine ability as a ball handler— and he was perfect coming off the bench.

Going into the season I had a clear game plan, but the burden would be on the players to perform the way I wanted them to. I planned to use four forwards—Bill Bradley and Dave DeBusschere backed by Cazzie Russell and Dave Stallworth who were like second team forwards. Bill Hosket and Donnie May would be guys at the far end of the bench and wouldn't play unless the game was over either way or we were in real foul trouble. Barnett and Frazier would handle the two starting guard positions and Mike Riordan's playing time would increase. In effect, that would give us a three-guard rotation.

Willis Reed was so powerful and such a workhorse that I knew all I had to do was give him a little blow here and there. Nate Bowman would back Willis up for those six or so minutes a game.

The roles of Hosket, May, Bowman, and Warren were very important. They had to go against the other players in the practices. Mike Riordan and John Warren had to play against Frazier and Barnett in the scrimmages and make Clyde and Dick work. That was very important for the team concept we developed. Cazzie Russell nicknamed the reserve players "Minutemen." They had to know all our plays backwards and forwards and be ready to come in and do an adequate job in place of a regular. The fringe guys are the ones who have to be ready when you need them. However, when they are not being used, their attitude can slide, and affect the team. On the other hand, you want to avoid complacency. So you don't want the guys bitching too much, and you don't want them bitching too little. It's an unsolvable problem for a coach.

I openly discussed how substitutions would be made. This let all the players know when they would be going out of a game and for how long. It helped them understand what was expected of them.

Some guys make it easy for a coach to substitute for them and put them on the bench. They're not the eager type, busting your chops to get into the game. They're very docile about it all and coaches subconsciously take those guys out of games more. And then there are other guys always just busting to get into the ballgame. They lie about how they feel, even hide an injury.

You can't sit there and worry about substitutions. You do what you think is right at the time—and you don't have much time. Based on history, based on experience, based on living with these guys, based on instincts and seeing the other guys, you substitute. Some of the substitutions might have seemed odd to some people who were watching the Knicks, but there was always a reason for what I did. There were times when I attempted to create a deliberate mismatch, resulting in the other team gaining an advantage. This made the other team try to capitalize on our handicap. Lots of times it would make them change things that had worked for them. A minus for us would then turn into a plus. And with intelligent players, if you made a substitution that seemed to handicap you, then your players would work harder to make up for things. My saying was "not to be handicapped sometimes is to be handicapped."

The future Hall of Famers, Bill Bradley, Dave DeBusschere, Walt Frazier, and Willis Reed were a little different. Those guys always wanted the ball when the game was on the line, they always played all out. They were aware of what they could do on the court at all times, and they could play with pain. However, all of them were secure enough about themselves and their role on the team, as well as intelligent enough to know how important they were to what we were doing, to say when they needed a break: "Hey, Red, take me out for a few minutes, give me a blow."

When that happened, no matter what the score was, no matter how good one of those guys was doing—bing—he was out of there. I'd never play those guys into exhaustion, and they were sensitive enough to know that it did them and the team no good to have them out there when they were dragging.

I used to talk to the guys at the end of the bench or just look them over carefully to see if they were in the game. "If you're not listening and watching," I would tell them, "you better act like you are—and you better be ready when we need you." Fortunately, our Minutemen were ready most of the time.

A case in point was Donnie May, who was married between exhibition games before the 1969–70 season began. Donnie came back without missing a dribble.

"Hey, Red, why don't you play Donnie 48 minutes tonight against Detroit," suggested DeBusschere after May came back from his short honeymoon. I didn't play May one minute that night. I had pity on him.

I had worked the guys hard in the 1969–70 pre-season. The results showed as we won our first five games and were clicking along. At San Francisco we lost a tough game 112–109, but then we started a new winning streak. We defeated the Detroit Pistons 116–92. And then we played the Bullets at the Garden.

In the last minutes of that game the crowd started roaring. They were making one hell of a racket. For a moment I didn't know what the commotion was about. I thought that perhaps there was a fight in the stands. Then I realized the fans were screaming for us to hold Baltimore under 100 points. We did. The final score was 128–99, moving our record to 7–1. Our defense was doing it for us.

"Let's go, Knicks. Let's go, Knicks. Dee-fense. Dee-fense." Opposing teams hated to hear those chants from our fans. They didn't like all the screaming aimed at keeping them under a hundred points. Holding other teams to under a hundred became a matter of pride for our fans and the players on the Knicks. It was their version of pitching a baseball shutout. We accomplished that "basketball shutout" 25 times that season—a record at that point in time.

The screaming never influenced my coaching. It gave the fans something to be interested in when a game was locked up early, but I was never that big on stats. I was bigger on results. If a player had a hard game, I'd take him out. I would never leave a tired guy in there just to hold another team to less than 100 points. But the 100-point goal did put pressure on our subs, who felt it from the regulars to hold the other teams under a hundred points. It gave the guys coming off the bench an extra incentive to play hard.

Our winning streak continued as we beat Milwaukee at the Garden and then racked up our seventh straight win in a game against Phoenix. We made it eight in a row with a victory over San Diego, giving that team its eighth straight loss.

L.A. was next. Although Jerry West was 18 for 18 from the foul line for the Lakers, we rolled past them for our ninth straight win.

We were 14–1 arriving in San Francisco to play the Warriors, the only team we had lost to so far that season. We had plenty of incentive to beat them—not to mention our desire to extend our winning streak to ten and break the record for the best NBA start—15–1.

Defense did it for us. We won the game 116–103, holding the fine shooting Warriors to just 18 points in the fourth quarter. DeBusschere played with a special protective contraption over a broken nose, but still managed to score 24 points and pull down a dozen rebounds.

In the locker room after the game Bradley announced: "It's a lot more fun rooming with Dave now. Before he broke his nose he used to snore all night. Now he's become much quieter."

The streak moved to 12 in a row with victories over Chicago and Boston. It was the Celtics' seventh straight loss of the season. Times had changed. Cincinnati was our next victim.

We escaped a big threat to beat Philly. That win against Philadelphia was particularly satisfying. We had a two-point lead with five seconds left in the game, and they had the ball and called a time-out.

"Either Hal Greer or Billy Cunningham will get the ball on the inbounds," I told our guys in the huddle. "I have a hunch that it'll be Greer at his spot, the head of the foul circle."

Philly inbounded. Bradley left his man and raced to Greer's spot.

Bill got his hand up just in time to deflect Greer's shot. And our streak was still alive.

Our fifteenth straight came against Phoenix at the Garden. Connie Hawkins of the Suns bitched: "My ankles, my arms, my wrists, and even my face is tired after playing against Reed, DeBusschere, and Stallworth."

Jerry West scored 41 points, but we wore down the Lakers at the Garden for number sixteen. And on Thanksgiving Eve in Atlanta the whole team was psyched for number seventeen—a win that would tie us with the Celtics of 1959 and Washington's 1946 team for the most consecutive wins in NBA history.

Before the game Atlanta's Bill Bridges went one-on-one verbally with Dick Barnett.

"You guys ain't gonna tie any record against us tonight," Bridges bragged.

"What's the matter," Dick popped back. "Ain't you guys going to play?"

The Hawks played, but we soared, winning the game 138–108. The press was calling me a "push-button coach," claiming all I had to do was make out a lineup card and we'd win. And that game was one of the reasons. The team was clicking—playing intelligent basketball, helping out, pressing, hitting the open man. Media coverage was intensive, and some people thought we'd never lose a game again.

Our eighteenth straight win showcased our defense and set an NBA record. It came against the Cincinnati Royals in a game played in the old Cleveland arena. Even though we were down 105–100 with 22 seconds left in the game, I didn't give up and neither did any of my players; we weren't going anywhere anyway until the game ended.

Six seconds left, and we were down by three points. Willis hit two foul shots. We were down 105–104 after Dave DeBusschere intercepted an inbounds pass and made a lay-up.

Cincinnati's player-coach Bob Cousy replaced Oscar Robertson, who had fouled out. Cousy got into trouble trying to inbound a pass, so he had to call a time-out, the last time-out Cincinnati had. In the huddle I told our guys we had nothing to lose by gambling and overplaying the logical receivers. We knew exactly what to do when we overplayed; each guy on the team had to compensate. Cousy's inbounds pass was stolen by Walt Frazier as the ball was smacked around in a scramble. Walt took a shot and was fouled. Coolly, he went to the line. He made both foul shots. We won the game 106–105.

In our dressing room later, guys were jumping for joy that the winning streak was intact. Across the way, the Royals were disappointed. They had had a great chance to beat us, and couldn't do it. Tom Van Arsdale of the Royals moaned: "It's like the gods are with them. It's like a nightmare." For us it was no dream. It was the result of good habits ingrained, all the practice sessions, all the confidence of coming back in so many games. The win put our record at 23–1.

The next night was different. We lost to Detroit at Madison Square Garden in what was a letdown for the team after the high of 18 straight wins, the comeback against Cincinnati, and all the media attention. Throughout that streak every team we played wanted to be the one to stop us if they could. And our guys developed supreme confidence in everything they were doing—steals, double-teaming, pressure defense, hitting the open man.

"Any game we're down even ten points going into the fourth quarter we can still win," Willis Reed told the press. That statement captured the spirit of the team.

The hundreds and hundreds of drills and my screaming of "See the ball, see the man" had made things almost automatic on defense. On offense I stressed their being able to see what they could take from how they were being played: tight, loose, where they were being picked up on the court, the flow of the other team from its offense to defense.

The guys were thrilled with the backing of the fans who lifted us up at Madison Square Garden. In the stands it was a regular melting pot: New York City cabbies and stockbrokers, garment center workers and cops, celebrities and college students. Celebrities who were basketball junkies included Dustin Hoffman, Elliott Gould, author William Goldman, and Peter Falk, who always had to be told to put out his cigar because they didn't allow smoking in the arena.

Woody Allen was a rabid Knick fan and used to come to the games with Diane Keaton. She was beautiful, like a china doll with porcelain skin. Woody was always trying to travel incognito. A big, bulky scarf was wrapped around his neck and part of his face, and big glasses covered what was visible of his face. His clothing was early Salvation Army. As an actor Woody Allen is a genius—but he was a hell of a bust at traveling incognito.

There was always lots of noise, lots of excitement, all kinds of things going on in the seats, but I didn't turn around too much to see what was going on. I concentrated on each exchange down the court. They were all like little battles. The only time I might have relaxed was on offense. Then I didn't look at the ball, but at the players off the ball to see if they had positioned themselves properly and set their men up. On defense I watched the positioning of our players in relation to how we were playing, what the score was, how much time was left in the game, and what the foul situation was for each team.

Every time the other team moved the ball on offense, a counter-move had to be made by our players on defense. I watched to see if they were guarding the passing lanes properly, if our guy guarding the man with the ball was exerting enough pressure, if our four other defenders were in position to adjust to offensive moves, poised to rebound, or to help out in a double-team. Positioning, anticipation, aggressiveness—all of these were things I looked for.

I was especially concerned that our guys not reach in on defense to try to steal the ball, and perhaps pick up a silly foul. I frowned on that and always wanted steals to come on the attempted pass.

Easy baskets by the opposition, transition baskets from their defense to their offense were things we had the power to prevent. I stressed this on defense a great deal, talked about it in practices, and had our players work on it against each other. In basketball there's a tendency for the team that scores to relax just a bit before getting back on defense. That's when they get exploited by easy baskets.

I spent many hours looking at films, trying to pick up any little insights I could—things that could give us a bit of an advantage. Ours was a set team with set rotations, but each player was ready to assume a role. One play that worked well was a forward-guard interchange. I would call an "X" with a play and the forward would assume the guard's role and vice versa. If you pulled that today, you'd have the Keystone Kops out there. Fortunately, I had guys who were well-schooled enough to handle that stuff.

From football I borrowed the two-minute drill. It was a way of getting all the guys to function quickly under pressure so we wouldn't waste time-outs. We knew exactly how to respond to presses and what the responsibility of each player was.

My innovation of the offense-defense switch also came into play in those two-minute drills. I spot-played one of our good shooters when our team was on the attack, and when we went back on defense I substituted with a player like Phil Jackson, whose long arms and knowledge of overplaying made him very effective. Phil welcomed his chance to slow down a hot offensive player.

I instilled in all of our players the knowledge that if they wanted to be stars, it was in their best interest to play team basketball. If they became a great team, then they'd each be recognized for their greatness. Team basketball meant not just the five guys playing on the court, but also the guys sitting on the bench, ready to contribute anytime they were called upon. Most players care a lot about individual stats. Our guys never cared once they saw team basketball working. They would look up at the statistical leaders and kid them. "Hey, we have nobody in the top five in scoring. We have no one among the rebounding leaders. Yet we are leading the league with the best record. We play team basketball. We win that way."

When it was working well, we represented what many people said was the most pleasing and greatest basketball team they ever saw. We were fluid and poised with all the parts contributing to the whole.

Our game style reminded me of the story about the insurance salesman who walked into a prospect's office.

"Hi, how are you doing? I'm here to sell you one hundred thousand dollars worth of insurance."

"Good," the prospect answered. "I'll take it."

"No. No! You can't take it yet," the insurance guy said. "I have to go through my check list first. You have to hear my sales pitch."

We never acted that way. If the other team gave us a shot, we took it right away. And if we were given an opening by the defense, we took it. We also made our own openings. We stressed being able to recognize instantly what the opposition gave us and being able to exploit it.

The way our guys set up the first offensive option usually worked. If it didn't work, we immediately went to the second option. There were never too many passes. A player was set up, came off a screen that was executed quickly and properly, and bang, bang—that was it.

If we hit the open man, it was usually in an area where he was skilled in shooting from. That's why our shooting percentage was good and why it looked so effortless. We planned it that way. Players worked with each other and for each other—to get free, to hit the open man, to box out. There were also set plays specifically designed for individual players.

One play that I tailored for Bradley typified our team play and the way we took advantage of Bill's talent, in this case his ability to move without the ball and get his shot off. Dick Barnett would inbound the ball at half court, usually from the left to Frazier. Bradley would set up in the far right-hand corner near the baseline. Willis would be at the edge of the foul circle while Dave DeBusschere would take up space on the left side of the court. When Barnett and Frazier came down toward the basket, Dave would move along the foul line and position himself to the right of it. From that spot he'd set a pick for Bill, who would rush by Dave and try to brush his man into him. At the same time Willis would move into position to the left of the foul line pretty close in to the basket.

If Dave's man switched off to take Bill, then Bill would continue along the baseline to the left and try to run Dave's man into Willis's pick.

One way or another we set things up so that Bill could hit his open shot 20 feet or so from the baseline. When all the guys executed properly, and they usually did, bingo! We had two points.

That's what was so pleasing about the team. Fans like to see players pass the ball intelligently and achieve easy shots, nice shots. Fans like to see a defense that traps, that makes steals, that anticipates, that helps out. Stats for defense have been popularized only in recent years. Defense had been an art that was unrewarded, unpublicized. We changed that.

One of the problems with that winning streak was that I was losing the low profile I had worked so hard to maintain. I wasn't just losing it—it was being forcibly removed. Back home in Cedarhurst, I had always been able to go into the Chinese laundry, the butcher shop, the candy store, and be treated just like any other guy in the neighborhood.

Now people who knew nothing about basketball were asking me
how long the streak would last, were offering me good luck charms,
and tons of free advice. That was the easy part. The tough part was the
phone calls from people in the neighborhood. Some of them were
congratulatory but others were invitations. Guys were insistent that I
come over and have dinner with them, that I appear before a local
elementary school class. They even had the topic picked out: "The
Secrets of Winning Basketball and Its Application to Life." I took a
raincheck on all invitations and used my old buddy Eddie Gottlieb's
line: "I'll get back to you."

One Sunday morning Selma and I were awakened at about seven. I
crawled out of bed and stumbled to the front door. That was my first
mistake. It wasn't the newspaper delivery. It was a bunch of kids.

My second mistake was opening the door. "What do you want?" I
asked in the grumpiest voice I could manage at that hour.

"We're here for autographs," the fattest and tallest of the kids said.

"Don't you know what time it is?"

"Yeah," the kid answered. "Don't you?"

"It's too early for autographs," I told them, trying to let them
down easy. "Please come back later."

"No, Red," the smallest of the kids squeaked. "We want the
autographs now. We want to do some trading later."

I counted heads. There were only five kids. I figured I'd sign
quickly and then get back to sleep.

"Okay, form a line, and I'll take care of you."

They lined up. The tallest kid, the ringleader, was first, and the rest
were in size places in descending order. The fat kid stuck five index
cards in my hand.

"What's this for?"

"Five autographs."

"Why five?"

"To keep one and trade the other four, maybe for a Walt Frazier or
a Bill Bradley."

I signed five times for each of them, waved good-bye, shut the
front door, and climbed back into bed, but just before I fell off to sleep
I realized anonymity had its rewards and fame had its problems.

* * *

After the loss to Detroit and the end of our winning streak, we were scheduled to play Seattle at the Garden. Before the game started I must have hung back in the locker room doing my pacing even more than usual. Realizing I was a little late, I rushed out and was starting to cut across the court to the Knick bench.

"Hey, buddy, where do you think you're going?" A burly usher I had never seen before barred my way.

"I'm going to the Knick bench."

"You can't go there. The game is about to start."

"But I'm Red Holzman, I'm the coach."

"That's a likely story."

"It's no story. Don't you recognize me?"

"No. I don't recognize you. And besides, a little squirt like you could never be the coach of the New York Knickerbockers!"

I got a big kick out of that exchange. It told me that I could still hide in a crowd.

"Okay, buddy," I kidded the usher. "If I can't go out there and coach, I'm going to leave right now and go to the movies."

"That's the best idea you've had yet, mister. So long."

I made a quick turn, faking a grand exit, when some fans who realized what was happening came to the rescue and identified me.

"Gee, Mr. Holzman." The usher was shaken. "I should have known. I'm sorry."

"No need to be sorry," I told him. "No harm done. You were just doing your job."

I shook the guy's hand and then went out there and did my job, coaching the team to a 129–100 win over Seattle. That brought our record to 24–2.

Willis Reed teased me afterward. "You've got us playing like a machine. Maybe the usher had it right, Red. You could have taken the night off, and we still would have won."

We won a lot that year, winding up with just 22 losses and 60 victories, the most by any Knick team ever. We could have won 65 to 67 games, but the last month of the season the players seemed not to be getting up as a team. We suffered defeats in some games that we should have won. We lost the last five games of the season, and were blown out by 50 points in our final regular season game by Portland, one of the weaker teams in the league.

Coaches find things to worry about—it's the nature of the business—and that year I was concerned that the team was losing some momentum just as we were heading into the playoffs.

Our first opponent was Baltimore, and I was even concerned about the weather. In April it's pretty nice in Maryland, and I didn't want my players dreaming about golf courses and beaches or laying down under trees.

The Bullets matched up very well against us. Jack Marin was a tough opponent for Bill Bradley. Gus Johnson had the strength to go against Dave DeBusschere. Wes Unseld and Willis Reed were two of the strongest guys in the league. And Walt Frazier versus Earl Monroe was a standoff. Since the matchups were so close, I spent a lot of time reminding our players to concentrate on helping out on defense.

Baltimore's Earl Monroe was a genuine superstar with an amazing shot-making ability. When Earl was on his game, he was all spins and bobs, stutter steps, blind passes, reverse feints, and invented shots thrown from anyplace on the floor.

We knew we had to contain Earl, but we knew we couldn't get to the point of worrying just about him and then getting killed by the other guys on Baltimore.

We beat the Bullets in the first game in double overtime at Madison Square Garden and made it two in a row with a seven-point win in Baltimore. Mike Riordan was a big help offensively, and we shut them down in the fourth quarter, outscoring them by 13 points.

Maybe the 2–0 lead and the fact that we had lost only twice in Baltimore in the last 15 games we had played against the Bullets made our guys a bit complacent. The Bullets came back, taking the next two games. In the third game Wes Unseld pulled down 34 rebounds, four more than our entire team. And Kevin Loughery took off the corset that protected his punctured lung, came back into action, and gave Baltimore a tremendous emotional lift. The fourth game was the "Earl Monroe Show" as the Pearl put on a clinic, making all kinds of incredible shots.

In the fifth game Willis played in pain with banged-up knees, but he came through in a great big way for us, scoring 36 points and taking down 36 rebounds. We blew Baltimore away, 101–80, holding them to just 11 points in the last quarter.

The sixth game was a defensive struggle, and our shooting was a little off. They had a big 30-point third quarter, and we wound up losing 96–87.

Going into the seventh game against the Bullets worried me. I knew that overall we had the better team, but I was concerned about Earl Monroe. I knew that last game could turn into Earl Monroe against Walt Frazier, superstar versus superstar, not the Knicks against the Bullets. Those were equal odds, but not the kind of odds a coach likes. Getting into that kind of position with the game on the line erases any kind of edge you may have built up.

The crowd at Madison Square Garden gave us a tremendous ovation; they were on their feet as the game started. Dave Stallworth raised his arms in the air and was like a cheerleader for the fans. There was so much noise that it was like the buzzing at a hockey game.

I had been concerned about Monroe, and he showed me I was right, scoring 32 points in the game. Fortunately, our depth was able to offset him. Dick Barnett scored 28 points and Walt Frazier had 15 plus ten assists. Cazzie Russell off the bench popped in 18 points in 21 minutes. We won 127–114.

It was a very tough series against a very tough team, and I think it helped our players get back into their mid-season groove. Just the thing they needed after coasting at the end of the year.

Milwaukee was next. They had an excellent coach in Larry Costello and an excellent assistant coach in Hubie Brown. Their team had a lot of starting talent but lacked our depth.

The Bucks also had Kareem Abdul-Jabbar, known at the time as Lew Alcindor. He was an imposing presence, but luckily Willis had the strength to move him out of position. The rest of our team also matched up very well against Milwaukee. We took the series four games to one.

Los Angeles, our opponent in the championship series, had an amazing team, including three-fifths of the league's first string All-Star team: Jerry West, Elgin Baylor, and Wilt Chamberlain. We knew it was going to be tough.

The people in New York City were just like family to the Knicks. Although those fans were rough on us at times, they helped us win a lot of games that 1969–70 season. They never gave up and never walked out of the Garden before a game was over, no matter what the score was.

Just once before had the Knicks reached the final round of the NBA playoffs. That was in 1951, when my Rochester team beat them. The Knicks had never won an NBA championship, and the fans were hungry for one. I really wanted to bring a title to New York City by beating the Lakers—a team many considered the best in the NBA. I worried throughout the whole series about making a mistake with a silly substitution, or having the team practice too long, or not enough, or forgetting to use a player.

Game one, played at Madison Square Garden, was a showcase for Willis Reed. I had told Willis to stay outside, to draw Wilt away from the boards. Wilt wouldn't budge, and Willis had his outside shot working. We were able to get off to a 25–12 lead, and then increase it to 50–30. The Lakers fought back in the closing minutes of the half, and we went into the locker room leading 65–54. With about nine minutes left in the third quarter, West and Baylor were pouring it on, and the Lakers led by three points.

But that was it for the Lakers. We swung the ball and tightened up on defense and won the game 124–112.

Willis wound up with 37 points, 16 rebounds, and five assists. Wilt had only 17 points and he missed nine of ten free throws. The key to the game was Chamberlain. He wouldn't come out and play tough defense, but I knew that wouldn't last.

It's strange, but a team that loses the first game of a series usually winds up with the edge in the second game. The team that wins the first game gains confidence in what it's doing and doesn't want to change anything. The losing team will make adjustments. It's like a boxing match. A guy goes back to his corner after losing a round and his cornerman says: "Hey, you had your left hand down all the time in that round. You're not protecting yourself. Next round make sure you keep your left hand up."

In the National Basketball Association there are great coaches who know the game inside out and study the films. They evaluate what takes place from game to game, and they adjust. Coaches are like cornermen in boxing giving advice. If those coaches have players who can follow their advice and adjust, their teams can win.

In the second game the Lakers adjusted and beat us, taking away our home court advantage. Wilt Chamberlain denied the middle and their outside people didn't allow us the perimeter shot as much as they had in the first game. They forced us to drive into closed-off areas.

It was good strategy for them and excellent coaching by Joe Mulaney. Reed had 29 points in the game—ten more than Wilt. The difference was Wilt, taking away a lot of our drives down the middle. West also was magnificent with 34 points. The final score was 105–103, Lakers.

The third game of the series was played in L.A. The Lakers had a tremendous first half. Jerry West had a hot hand, and Elgin Baylor gave Wilt a lift on the boards. At the half they led us 56–42.

In the second half I had our players go back to the tactics they had used in the first game of the series—outside perimeter shooting. We hit ten third-quarter outside shots while the Lakers made only one. The lead swung back and forth, back and forth. It was frantic.

With 50 seconds left in regulation time, Willis Reed's free throw gave us a one-point lead, 98–97. With 38 seconds left, Jerry West hit a jump shot, giving the Lakers a one-point lead. With 18 seconds left, Dick Barnett banged in an 18-foot off-balance shot and gave us a one-point lead.

The Lakers called their last time-out. Both teams huddled to go over strategy. I told our guys to foul Wilt Chamberlain as soon as he got the ball. "We'll take a chance," I said.

Although Los Angeles was in the penalty situation, I was willing to take the gamble, given the way Chamberlain shot free throws. Wilt made one of two and the score was tied at 100 with 13 seconds left in the game.

With three seconds left, DeBusschere popped in a jump shot and everybody thought the game was over. Wilt, disgusted, just flipped the ball inbounds to Jerry West, who heaved a desperation 55-foot shot. Incredibly, the shot went in. One more amazing feat for Jerry West.

Chamberlain was halfway to the Laker locker room when West's shot went in. They had to call him back onto the floor.

We were all stunned for a moment, but reality is reality. The game was going into overtime. No way we were going to lay down and quit.

Dick Barnett spoke for our guys when he said, "Aw, man, let's forget it."

It was an appropriate comment. We couldn't do anything about West's shot. We had to put it behind us, keep on playing, and try to win the game in OT. Dick Barnett's shot with just four seconds left in the overtime gave us a 111–108 win.

Willis Reed was the big man again as far as stats—38 points, 17 rebounds, but the other guys, the parts of the whole, had also done their jobs. Dave DeBusschere scored 21 points and pulled down 15 rebounds. Clyde had 19 points, 7 assists, while Barnett had 18 clutch points.

That overtime victory gave us back the home court advantage, and it was a crucial edge. Even if L.A. won the fourth game, the whole thing would become a three-game series, best two out of three, and two of those games would be played at Madison Square Garden.

Dick Barnett picked up in game four where he left off in game three. In the first quarter he made six of seven outside shots. The Lakers, with Baylor leading the way, stayed right with us and then got a little ahead. They led 54–47 at the half. With eight minutes left in the game, Barnett's shot tied the score at 79. Back and forth it went as we kept trading baskets with the Lakers. With 23 seconds left in regulation time, Elgin Baylor tied the score at 99. Once again we had to go into overtime.

L.A. used forward John Tresvant for the first time in the series. He helped them a lot in the OT. They beat us 121–115.

That was the first game in the series that we were out-rebounded. It was clear to me that Willis was a little tired, while Chamberlain seemed to be getting stronger. Wilt had 18 points and 25 rebounds, and played strong defense in that fourth game.

With the series all tied up, the fifth game was played at the Garden on May 4. Chamberlain moved the Lakers off to a good start, making three baskets in less than two minutes. They led 11–4. Then they led 25–15, and things got worse. Willis Reed drove down the left side of the lane for a lay-up and fell to the floor. The Garden crowd was stunned and silent. The prognosis was that Willis had strained a couple of muscles in his right thigh. No one knew how serious it was, but Willis had to be taken out of the game.

I remembered a game earlier in the year when we had played San Francisco, and Nate Thurmond had been tossed out by the refs. We relaxed. Then they regrouped and won the game without their big man. Psychologically they did more and we did less. I realized that when you get handicapped like that, the other team is aware of it and you're aware of it. Sometimes you do more, and they do less.

I put in Nate Bowman to replace Willis Reed, but the Lakers went again and again to Wilt, who scored seven of L.A.'s next 12 points. With their lead 37–24, I replaced Bowman with Bill Hosket, but that didn't help too much. Their lead was 43–32, with less than five minutes remaining in the half. I then switched DeBusschere onto Wilt. Although Dave gave away eight inches and a lot of beef, I figured his toughness, mobility, and the other guys helping out would be worth something.

At the half we trailed 53–40. Wilt had 18 points and 12 rebounds. No Knick had even five rebounds or ten points. It didn't look too good for us, but I knew we had been in similar situations before, that the guys were disciplined, that they had a lot of heart. All the practice and repetitions, all the training and teamwork were still part of what we were.

Willis had taken a couple of shots of cortisone but he couldn't play. He was the league's Most Valuable Player and his not being there was a tremendous loss, but I believed we could do it without him. It wasn't my way to give pep talks in the locker room at the half, but this time I did.

"Willis has won a lot of games for us this season," I told the guys. "Let's win this one for Willis." I turned my attention to DeBusschere. "Dave, you shoot outside against Wilt. Draw him away from the boards."

"Anything you think will work, Coach, I'll do," Dave said.

"Any suggestions any of you other guys have?" I asked.

"I think we should try a zone offense," Bradley volunteered. "Let's try a one-three-one zone. That might be effective."

I agreed with Bradley. It was a very good idea. "We'll do it," I told them. "Give a lot of defensive pressure, help out inside as much as you can, block out. We still have a chance to win this thing."

I started the second half with a three forward offense—Cazzie Russell, Dave DeBusschere, and Bill Bradley, with Frazier and Barnett at the guard positions. I had my five best outside shooters on the floor as a unit. Four minutes into the third quarter we chopped their lead to five points, but then fell back to trail by 11.

When the fourth quarter began we were down by seven. Willis was on a dressing table in the locker room listening to the game, and the crowd was demoralized when the announcement was made that he would not return to action.

A couple of minutes into the fourth quarter we cut the L.A. lead to three points and the crowd got involved, as involved as I ever heard it at Madison Square Garden.

"Let's go, Knicks, let's go, Knicks." The chant kept getting louder and louder.

"They aren't 19,500 spectators," Bradley said. "They are 19,500 participants."

DeBusschere picked up his fifth foul, and I put Dave Stallworth in to replace him. "Stalls," I told Dave, "don't let Wilt feel you. Get off him. If he feels you, he knows exactly where you are and he likes that."

Wilt was the strongest man in the world, and he outweighed Stallworth by almost 80 pounds, but with his quickness Dave did a hell of a job of keeping daylight between him and Wilt. Dave was even able to steal the ball coming around on the pass into Chamberlain. And that threw Wilt off.

A Barnett jumper and a Stallworth basket tied the game at 89–all. I had told the guys to shoot from outside to pull Chamberlain out—they were doing it and they were hitting.

Those final minutes of the fourth quarter were like an old-time movie speeded up—our guys scrambling, popping from outside, Frazier's quick hands darting in for steals, and the roar of the crowd, the stamping of feet, the squeaking of sneakers back and forth on the Garden floor. Walt Frazier's final shot of the game clinched our 107–100 win.

That fourth quarter had been a terrific team effort. We had

outscored the Lakers 32–18, made no turnovers, and forced them into ten of their 30 game turnovers. Chamberlain scored only four points in the second half, and Jerry West didn't get a field goal. The Lakers were dazed by what we did. We made it tough for them to get the ball up the court, and they took only 66 shots all game—about 30 below their normal pace. We got 103 shots.

That fifth-game victory bought time for us and gave us hope.

Willis was unable to play at all in the sixth game in Los Angeles, a game in which the Lakers adjusted and we had a letdown. They used Dick Garrett outside, and he made some good shots which made it difficult for us to collapse around Wilt, who scored 45 points and pulled down 27 rebounds. He stuck it to us.

Both teams flew back to New York City for the seventh and final game of what had been a hell of a series. New York versus Los Angeles attracted tremendous media attention. It had been a great season for me and the team. I knew, however, that if you've never won the championship, and get that close and lose—then it's a very loud thud. In basketball they judge you by the last thing you do.

It wasn't easy to play with so much excitement, so much coverage and attention all the time, but we had strong-minded guys on that team. I had stressed that they keep things in perspective when they became too happy over the many things we had to celebrate during the season. I had my eye on bringing a championship to New York City. And that was the goal I made all the players keep in mind.

The seventh game took place on Friday night, May 8, 1970. It was our thirty-eighth sellout of the season and the crowd was ready, but we weren't too sure about Willis Reed.

We'd been sweating all day long whether Willis would be able to play. Both teams were out on the floor warming up and Willis was being looked after by the doctors in the dressing room. I waited with him to make sure he was all right. Although I wanted to win a championship, I didn't want to win it at the expense of a player. It was up to the doctors to give the okay for Willis to play, and it was up to Willis to say definitely whether he could play or not.

When the decision was finally made that Willis would play, I walked out onto the floor with him. The applause was tremendous. That image of the coach and his banged-up center coming out at the start of the seventh game couldn't have been more dramatic if it had been planned. It was even more exciting that it actually just happened that way.

Willis limped out on the floor and took some practice shots. Players on both teams just stopped what they were doing and stared. Our guys got all pumped up by the sight of him out there, and the L.A. guys were given a jolt. They never expected to see Willis there.

After about five minutes of practice, Willis came back to the bench. Dr. James Parkes, our team doctor, and I sat with him.

"There's still some soreness," Willis told me, "but I can do it."

"Swell, I'll start you."

"Go back in and get some more heat for that leg," Parkes advised Willis, "and get some rest."

Willis left, limped onto the runway, and I caught sight of Selma. She was wearing the same orange and beige horizontal-striped knit dress she had worn to each of our playoff games for the past six weeks.

"If the team can't have Willis," she had kibitzed when we had driven into the Garden earlier in the day, "then maybe the dress will bring good luck."

At 7:41 John Condon got on the mike to give the crowd our starting lineup. When DeBusschere and Bradley were introduced, it set the crowd to cheering. When Condon announced: ". . . At center, Captain Willis Reed," the fans stood and roared and roared, and the roof in the Garden trembled. That racket went on for almost a minute. It was a good thing Condon still had to introduce Frazier and Barnett. That made the crowd quiet enough so we could hear ourselves think. But even though they sat down, they were up all the way.

Willis and Chamberlain lined up for the tap-off. Wilt went high and Willis barely left his feet—he couldn't. L.A. got the tap. Baylor missed a jump shot from the side. Dave DeBusschere rebounded and we moved out on offense.

Willis was the last man downcourt, moving with a kind of pegleg skip. He set up behind the foul line and Wilt dropped off him. Flat-footed, Willis hit a 15-footer. We led 2–0.

And the crowd was roaring.

Ninety seconds later we had a 3–2 lead. Willis set up in the right corner about 20 feet from the basket. Again Chamberlain dropped off him. Frazier fed Willis, who shot and hit. The crowd went wild and so did the guys on our bench.

By hitting a couple of baskets at the start, Willis helped get us off. He also gave us a tremendous lift and brought the crowd into the game early. There was so much shouting and jumping that I could have sworn the Garden was moving.

A minute later we were up 9–2, and the Lakers called a time-out. Our non-starters leaped off the bench with their fists in the air. They swarmed all over the regulars when they came back to the bench.

We led 15–6, then 30–17. We were up by six at the quarter. We had a 27-point lead at the half and were up by 25 going into the third quarter.

L.A. scored 30 in the fourth quarter when we were kind of coasting with a big lead. I knew it was impossible to keep a great team like Los Angeles down forever.

Heading into the last six minutes we had a 106–81 lead, and the fans were going crazy. They were standing up, screaming over and over again: "We're number one! We're number one! We're number one!"

As the coach I couldn't stop and be happy the way some of the players could. They thought the game was over. I knew from experience that anything could happen. I knew it was tough to keep the pressure on L.A. because our guys had played a lot of minutes and built a big lead. I knew the shot clock could create a problem and that if we didn't score and they did, the game could become close in a hurry.

With just a few seconds left in the game some of our guys were so excited they wanted to run out on the floor. I had to restrain them. I wanted to make sure everything was done properly, because until it was all over, there was nothing to celebrate.

At the end, 19,500 fans were on their feet. We beat the Lakers 113–99, bringing the first NBA championship in history to New York City.

Selma spent that game in her customary seat behind the visitor's bench. She didn't sit there to pick up any opposition secrets, but rather so she wouldn't be too close to me. She never liked to hear all my screaming at the players and refs. My daughter Gail, my cousin Harry, and a group of friends, including some from Puerto Rico, sat with

Selma that night and helped make up that cheering section. When the game ended, the Garden was bedlam. The Knick players and I were escorted off the floor by security officers. Some of those fans were so happy that all they wanted to do was whack us on the back, and a few got in some good shots despite the police protection.

In the pandemonium Selma bumped into Dustin Hoffman who was very excited about the championship. "Selma, do you think you can manage to get me into the locker room to congratulate Red and the players?" he asked.

"If I can get you through all these people, you might have a chance, Dustin," she told him.

The two of them worked their way through celebrating Knick fans down under the court floor and into the locker room area. Selma spotted the head of security, whom she knew.

"Is it okay for this man to go in and congratulate Red and the players?"

The very tall security man looked down at Dustin. "Who's this guy?"

"Dustin Hoffman," Selma answered.

"What's he got to do with basketball?"

"Nothing, really, he's an actor," Selma answered.

"But I sometimes play basketball," Dustin cut in, and gave the security guy one of his big smiles.

"All right," the guard said. "Go in, but don't stay too long."

I have a vague memory of Dustin coming in and shaking my hand and doing his Cazzie Russell imitation amid the popping champagne bottles and the bear hugs and the screams of "We did it, we did it" that filled the locker room.

I enjoyed the horseplay, the excitement, all the media attention, and well-wishers. Even Wilt Chamberlain came in and shook my hand, and offered his congratulations. It was like a three-ring circus. I tried to stay in the background. Never one to get up front too much, I let the players grab the spotlight. They deserved it.

Nate Bowman kept squirting Dave Stallworth with champagne. Dave paid him no attention. Stallworth had played his part in the victory and he was dizzy from the whole experience. He told a reporter what he thought of Willis.

"There was no way Reed could play. He was limping so bad. The guy is beautiful, just beautiful. To me personally, he showed so much guts. You got to go mad when a guy who ought to be in a wheelchair comes out there. Deep down in his heart Willis knew he shouldn't be out there, but he knew what his presence could do for us. He's a hell of a man."

Frazier told a reporter: "Just the presence of Willis was the turning point in the game. To see him come out, and when he made his two baskets . . . We were worried, man. A couple of guys tried to tell jokes before we came out but nothing was funny."

Willis Reed was the big story, not for what he did but for how he lifted and inspired the entire team. He played 27 minutes and scored only four points, but his being able to play enabled us to have a guy push Chamberlain out of position a little bit, and, more important, to take another four fouls at the center position. With Bowman also playing Chamberlain, we had six more fouls from the center position and were able to capitalize on Wilt's ineffective foul shooting.

Chamberlain did many things, but we knew foul shooting was not his strength and we capitalized on it. Wilt grabbed 24 rebounds in the game and scored 21 points but was 1–11 from the foul line. That was a very, very important factor in our win.

The psychological effect of what Willis did overshadowed others' achievements. Willis *was* tremendous, but what Walt Frazier did paid the rent. Clyde was sensational. His was the greatest effort in the most important game ever played by anybody on our team.

Walt was 12–12 from the foul line, 12–17 from the field, getting free for his shot over and over again, and scoring off steals. He had 19 assists and pulled down seven rebounds, which was not unusual for him because he was one of the great rebounding guards in NBA history. The only other thing Clyde could have done was to have sold tickets to the game. He was busy.

I was happy to celebrate and even happier to get away from the celebration. Lots of people place too much emphasis on the trimmings. The important thing was achieving what had seemed unachievable. The Knicks had been in business since 1946, and this was their first championship. It was a thrill to win one for the people of New York City.

Finally I managed to shake myself loose from the celebrants and the interviewers and met up with Selma and some friends from my basketball days in Puerto Rico. We had some drinks at the Penn Plaza Club and swapped old stories. Then Selma and I drove home to Cedarhurst, had some corned beef sandwiches, and watched the replay of the game on television. It was only then, seeing it all over again, that I was fully able to appreciate what had happened.

Winning the championship underscored the philosophy I always had that basketball is a team game, and if you don't play as a team, you're not going to win. The potential for team basketball was there in all of the players on the Knicks, waiting to be tapped. It was my good fortune to be the catalyst for all that talent.

The guys we had counted on all year were the guys that did it in that final game. Bradley and DeBusschere scored 35 points between them. Dave had 18 points and 17 rebounds and had to tussle with Baylor. Frazier and Barnett had a total of 57 points and used up 86 of the 96 minutes at the guard position. The other ten minutes were played by Riordan to give breathers to Walt and Dick, who put out a lot of defensive pressure. L.A. had 23 turnovers compared to just 11 for us, so our double-teaming and press worked well. There were good minutes by Russell, Stallworth, and Bowman, who played 21 minutes and had six points and five rebounds.

In recognition for what we had accomplished, the team and I were invited to Gracie Mansion and given the key to the City of New York by Mayor John V. Lindsay. Bud Palmer, a former Knick, was the official greeter of New York City, and his excitement was great to see.

I was voted Coach of the Year in the National Basketball Association and got a kick out of that. That championship season had fringe benefits for everybody. The media attention was tremendous— and practically every player wrote a book telling his story about what had happened. And there was a big opportunity for commercials and endorsements. I always insisted that all the players be included in commercials, as well as Danny Whelan. We won it as a team; it was only right in my opinion that we do commercials as a team.

Bill Bradley was the only player who never did a commercial. He was very conscious even then of his image, and had a clause in his contract that said he did not have to do any endorsements. Instead of doing commercials, Bill did things in his own way, quietly, helping out kids and doing community service that the press and public never even knew about.

The advertising guys even got me into the act. I did a print ad for Antony and Cleopatra cigars and talked about Jerry West and the incredible 55-foot shot he made against us in the playoffs. I also did a radio skit with an actor for White Rose products. We told people to buy string beans, pears, and tomato sauce—all the company products that came in cans. I always thought I stumbled over the script they gave me to read, but the actor was good. He coached me through it all. I also did a voice-over on TV for the racing association.

The only endorsement I wish I had had an opportunity to make (and who knows, in those hectic post-championship days they may have tried to reach me) was for Dewar's scotch. As Selma and my good friends know, I do enjoy a drink now and then, and I've always been loyal to the label. (If you're reading this book, Mr. Dewar, it's still not too late!)

In early 1970 Eddie Donovan left the Knicks to help set up the new Buffalo NBA franchise. Things were moving along like clockwork on our team, and Ned Irish talked me into holding down both the coaching and general manager job, which was no problem. As the coach I knew the needs of the ball club better than anyone. As the general manager I was able to make deals, adjust the talent on the roster to the needs of the time, and reward the guys who did a lot of sacrificing, the team players. I always bent over backward for guys like Phil Jackson and Dick Barnett, who did things for the team that never appeared in the stat sheets—helping out on defense, giving up a good shot to a guy with a better shot, keeping the other players in the flow of the game, the instincts that drive a season.

Our 1969–70 season had been something special. Kids on the street imitated Walt Frazier and Bill Bradley. We had come back from big deficits in games and we had blown teams away. Pinpoint passing, steals, hot hands coming off the bench, team defense and offense flowing almost perfectly—all of these were part of that unforgettable season.

CHAPTER 3

As coach I was able to enjoy what had happened in that championship season all summer. As general manager I didn't have too much time to dwell on the victory. The draft was coming up, and then rookie camp and negotiations with players. I kept working. What little free time I had was spent around home or at the beach.

As general manager my routine was to arrive at my office at the Garden at about ten A.M. I would come off the elevator singing an off-key rendition of "Almost Like Being In Love" or "What a Difference a Day Makes." Somehow all kinds of characters managed to get into my office. There were guys peddling miracle cures for player ailments, ways to get players to grow extra inches. One man wanted to sell me pills to make our guys jump two inches higher. There were lots of letters full of coaching advice, and trading tips. I received medical, astrological, vegetarian and even religious advice, all unsolicited.

Hopeful applicants also came around, trying to convince me that they deserved to play for the Knicks. There was one guy I distinctly remember.

"Mr. Holzman, thank you, thank you, thank you," he began, "for giving me the opportunity to demonstrate my case." While he talked I was wondering what was taking the security people so long to get to my office.

"I want to play guard, Mr. Holzman. I can play better than Walt Frazier or Dick Barnett. And I'll sign with the Knicks for only $300,000 a year—a real bargain—I promise you."

"There's no room on the roster," I said, trying to let the guy down easy.

"When you see what I have to offer, you'll make room, Mr. Holzman. Not only can I play great basketball, but for no extra charge I'll dance at halftime."

With those words the guy broke into a soft-shoe routine, accompanying himself by whistling "Tea for Two." He showed some talent as a dancer, so I waited for him to finish up his little act.

"No encore today, please," I told the guy, who had worked up a bit of a sweat. "I have a lot to do, but I can see you have some ability." Then I took him gently by the arm, and walked him out of my office.

"Take this man's name and phone number for future reference," I told my secretary Gwynne Bloomfield. I shook the guy's hand.

"We'll call you if something turns up. Thanks a lot for dropping by."

"Thank you, Mr. Holzman, for letting me show my stuff." With those words he tap-danced his way out of the office, and, thankfully, out of my life.

At training camps guys always wanted tryouts. I'd tell them we had enough candidates or that the roster was full or that we had no more money left, attempting to kid them out of their fantasies. Some of those people were a little dangerous, and a few would get belligerent.

"Whadayamean, I can't try out?" some of them would roar. "You gotta let me show what I can do. Where am I gonna go? What am I gonna do?"

They were frustrated. In most cases they did not care about playing basketball. They just wanted the good things that went with it. Some were envious that Walt Frazier had a fur coat and a Rolls Royce.

In one training camp I turned away a guy who had been really persistent about getting a tryout. Then I went about my business in the locker room. When I came out on the floor, the guy was back, this time out on the court in full Knick issue, going one-on-one against Mike Riordan. Somehow he had managed to talk himself into a "tryout." I booted him the hell out of there, but I allowed him to keep all the New York Knick issue, the socks, the jersey. He was such a finagler that I figured he had earned the stuff.

During one of our playoffs against Baltimore, a fat little kid about five six came in.

"Mr. Holzman," he said seriously, "I can play better than anybody you have on the team." The guy had some problems. You could see it. I tried to be nice to him.

"You can probably play really well," I told him, "but it wouldn't be fair to the guys who have been with us all year. They deserve to be playing in the playoffs. Maybe you'd better go and see Bob Ferry, the general manager of Baltimore. They might be able to use you."

"I don't know." He was starting to twitch.

"You really should. We have no room for you. Baltimore might have some room for you."

"Okay, Mr. Holzman, if you put it that way," he said.

I wondered whether it was my logic or the fact that he was a Baltimore fan that led him to his decision. Whatever, I was happy to see him go.

Sure enough, that night I saw him walking into the arena with the Baltimore team. Those guys have a knack for getting into buildings. Then I noticed the guy was headed straight for me.

"Mr. Holzman, Bob Ferry said for me to come back to you. He said you need me more than he does."

"Well, we're on opposite teams," I began, "and it would be unfair of me to take you on just now, and there are all kinds of rules against it, even though, if you want to know the truth, there might not be a problem with doing that, if you get my point." My imitation of Casey Stengel (or was it my smile?) seemed to be working. The guy kept nodding.

"Give me a call after the playoffs and we'll see what we can do about next year."

"You've got a deal, Mr. Holzman, but only if Baltimore can't use me. You know that's my team." We shook hands. I must admit I had a few nervous moments after the playoffs, and the first time we played

The gang's all there—the 1945–46
Rochester Royals National League Champs.

The Rochester Royals scouting Mae West.

Saturday night Royals fever at
the Edgerton Park Arena in Rochester.

ROCHESTER ROYALS NBA 1950-51
BACK L.to R.
CALHOUN, McNAMEE, RISEN, COLEMAN, JOHNSON
FRONT L.to R.
DAVIES, WANZER, HOLZMAN, NOEL, SAUL

The 1950–51 NBA Champs—Rochester Royals.

George Mikan (l) and some
of the boys whooping it up.

Three Royal guards: Al Cervi
(r), Bob Davies (c), and me.

In the early days with the
workmen's circle.

PAUL A. GLUCKSTERN

Wedding bells.

Doctor Selma, baby Gail, and patient Red.

Red Holzman night in Rochester,
with my two favorite women: Selma (l) and
my mother (r), circa 1950.

My former coaches Les Harrison (l)
and Nat Holman (r).

Happy days in
St. Louis with my old
boss Ben Kerner.

Willis going
for two!

Bill Bradley,
always moving.

Willis Reed,
always wanting the ball
in the clutch.

Dick Barnett—
airborne—"Fall
back, Baby!"

Walt Frazier
vs. Jerry West—two
of the best.

The "Pearl"
executing one of his
"makeup" shots.

Clyde over
Wilt—a lot to
get over.

Dave DeBusschere—the
open man—letting
it go.

Ned Irish, Howard Cosell, Willis Reed, me,
and Irving Mitchell Felt, after
the first championship.

It ain't over till it's over!

The winning moment—May 8, 1970—and I'm still working.

WORLD CHAMPIONS
1969-70 NEW YORK KNICKERBOCKERS
Standing (left to right)—Coach William (Red) Holzman, Phil Jackson, Dave Stallworth,
Dave DeBusschere, Capt. Willis Reed, Bill Hosket, Nate Bowman,
Bill Bradley, Chief Scout Dick McGuire, and Trainer Dan Whelan.
Seated (left to right)—John Warren, Don May, Walt Frazier, President Ned Irish, Chairman
of the Board Irving Mitchell Felt, General Manager Ed Donovan,
Dick Barnett, Mike Riordan, and Cazzie Russell.

PHOTO BY GEORGE KALINSKY

New York City Hall
with Mayor Lindsay—celebrating the
second championship in 1970.

PHOTO BY GEORGE KALINSKY

Selma, Dustin Hoffman,
and me in a light moment
celebrating the 1969–70
Knick championship.

Bill Bradley's last hurrah
and my first hurrah.

November 17, 1977, a nostalgic moment:
the Franklin K. Lane High School Gymnasium named for me.

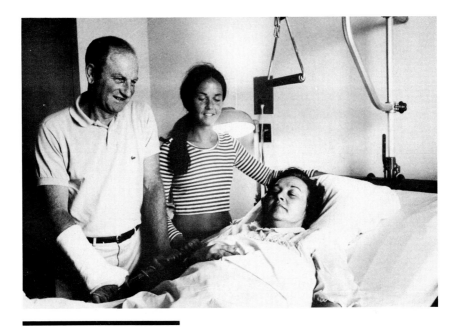

Tough days after the accident.

Hard at work as
G.M.—playing hurt!

Springfield, Massachusetts, Hall of Fame
induction dinner lineup: Tommy Heinsohn, Commissioner
David Stern, me, and Billy Cunningham.

SPRINGFIELD
∴
OR BUST !

Posing nicely with my daughter, Gail,
at the Springfield Hall of Fame
festivities.

Fuzzy Levane—
always on my side!

"I'll give you if you give me."
With the master, Red Auerbach.

I didn't always play
against 80-year-old ladies—here
I am getting congratulated by Martina.

Selma and me nowadays—a couple
of fans in the stands.

Baltimore the following year. But now, nearly two decades later, I think I can relax.

Dealings with agents gave me a few rough moments too. One of the predictable lines they used about a player cut from another team and trying to sign with the Knicks was: "He was the last guy to be cut. He never got a fair deal." Funny, none of the agents ever seemed to represent a player who was the *first* guy cut.

Another approach many agents used was comparing their player to a great star. "If he were three inches taller, he'd be just like George Mikan," or "If he had just a bit more speed, he would be just like Walt Frazier," or "Once he is able to build himself up a little more, he'll be as strong as Dave Cowens." The line "Never kid a kidder" (or some variation) was always in my mind, but I never did insult an agent by using it.

There was a guy, I'll call him agent X. He represented a lot of players, including a rookie he claimed was the second coming of Oscar Robertson. When we finally were able to get the entire deal worked out and signed, I met with the player. I don't know what possessed me, but I decided to throw him a curve.

"Your agent told me all about you," I told the kid. "Now that all the legal stuff is over, tell me, can you play basketball?"

"Well, Mr. Holzman, I'm really not that good at it now, but if you teach me, I might be pretty good."

I called up the agent. "You son of a bitch," I screamed. "After all you told me about the greatness of the kid, now I have to first start teaching him!"

Good thing players don't negotiate their own contracts.

As we entered the 1970–71 season our roster was stripped of some of its depth in the expansion draft. Nate Bowman, Donnie May, and Bill Hosket went to Buffalo, and John Warren moved on to Cleveland. In their places were guys who wound up just filling in.

A big plus for us was the return of Phil Jackson from the disabled list after recovering from serious back problems. That year Phil was just getting back into the swing of things, and he played in 71 games, averaging about ten minutes a game. Always one of my favorite players, Phil would cause havoc defensively with his extra long arms and energetic elbows. He was very, very intelligent and knew all the plays. Phil's real forte was defense, and he could play anybody from a center to a guard and create all kinds of problems for them.

I had scouted Phil in college, at North Dakota, where he was a center and a pretty good scorer under Coach Bill Fitch. I saw a lot of potential in him even though he didn't look that effective in his senior year. However, I was aware that he had lost 20 pounds due to a virus. Other scouts didn't know this, and lots of them gave up on him as a prospect.

In the 1967 draft we had made Phil Jackson our number two pick right behind Walt Frazier. That summer, in my role as chief scout, I went to Williston, North Dakota to get Phil to sign his contract with the Knicks.

Phil was a small-town guy. He was teaching in a Christian camp in Williston and was very dedicated to his work. "I'm very pleased," Phil told me, "that the Knicks thought so highly of me to draft me, but I'm having some slight second thoughts. . . ."

"That's only natural, Phil. We all have them."

"Mr. Holzman," he continued, "my original plans were to attend graduate school and become a minister. I still think about that."

"I respect your frankness," I told Phil. "But you're a young guy with your whole life ahead of you. Sign with the Knicks now. I have the contract with me. You'll be playing out of a great city—New York—and you'll have a fine career. And when you're finished with pro ball, you'll still be young enough to do whatever you want to do."

I finally convinced him to give the Knicks and New York City a try.

"I guess I can count on you, Mr. Holzman, to help me over the rough spots in New York," Phil said.

"I'll be there," I told him. "You can count on that."

Later that summer the Knicks were getting set to start training camp for the 1967–68 season. Selma and I went to Kennedy Airport to pick up Phil Jackson who was reporting to the Knicks for the first time. He had never been to New York City before.

At the airport we waited for Phil to come out of the arrival gate. When he appeared, Selma was impressed. She had been around big basketball players before, but never ones with Phil's broad shoulders.

"It looks like they squeezed him into the suit jacket," she kidded, "and forgot to take the hanger out."

The three of us then squeezed into my Chevrolet and began the ride into the city. We were driving along Queens Boulevard on our way toward the Midtown Tunnel. Suddenly a kid threw a rock that smashed against the car's windshield. I was kind of pissed, especially since the rock made a little hole in the windshield. However, when you're in New York and you're in traffic, you keep on moving.

"Phil, sorry about the welcome wagon," I said, trying to make a joke out of the whole thing. "To quote Satchel Paige—'Don't look back, something may be gaining on you.'"

We all laughed. Despite this rocky start, Phil learned to love New York City and became one of the guys on the team who moved around Manhattan with no trouble at all.

A rugged individualist, Phil always liked to play games with my watch and sometimes it cost him dearly. If the team was leaving at 10:00, he would see how close to that minute he could cut it. One time he and Mike Riordan showed up at 10:03 and missed the bus from Allentown to Trenton. They didn't have enough money between them to rent a car and had to hitchhike to Trenton.

I laid them both out and fined them. "Not only are you going to do what I tell you, you're going to like doing it." Phil didn't smile and he didn't like it, but he pretty much followed all the team rules after that.

He was a hell of a ballplayer and another guy to whose advantage it was to play team basketball. He never had an agent. Functioning as general manager, I always tried to see to it that he was paid properly, and there were times when I would arrange for him to receive more money than he asked for. He was worth it.

In practices I always warned the guys to be extra cautious when Phil was warming up. Like a bull in a china shop with those long arms and legs windmilling about, Phil would come running out full of fire and enthusiasm, hit a guy with his shoulder or knock another guy on his ass or throw a pass to one of the guys when they weren't looking and the ball would hit the guy in the head. Phil never had any but the best of intentions, though, and his awkwardness was a source of good-natured kidding on the team.

A man for trends, Phil roomed for a time with Eddie Mast. They both had full dark beards and could've been featured in a Smith

Brothers Cough Drop ad. Other guys talked sports or fashions; Phil debated politics, philosophy, and religion. For a while he was a vegetarian, then he was sort of a "flower child." Danny Whelan nicknamed him "Hippie Phil." He read Freud, Nietzsche, and Marx, but Phil never flaunted it—he was one of the guys and spoke down to earth.

But in some ways Phil Jackson is still a man of mystery to me. He inscribed his book *Maverick* this way:

> To Red: Thanks for teaching me the game. I am still learning, however. I admired the method but sometimes questioned the role. Is it worth it working for the truth?

Every once in a while I pick up that book. I'm still trying to figure out what he meant.

The 1970 draft was conducted by conference call on March 30. (That's still another way the league has changed in my five decades there. Now there's a lot of hoopla, and the draft is televised and players are brought in to meet the media and the fans.) There was a lot of talent available in 1970. Detroit had the number one pick and took Bob Lanier. Rudy Tomjanovich went second to San Diego. Next Atlanta selected "Pistol Pete" Maravich, while Boston used its number four pick to take Dave Cowens. We had the last pick among the seventeen NBA teams and chose Mike Price, a quick guard from Illinois. Los Angeles selected the 64th player in the draft, George Mikan's son, Larry, out of the University of Minnesota. Another interesting trivia question: Who was selected 103rd in the 1970 NBA draft? The answer: Billy Paultz of St. John's, taken by San Diego.

Three more new teams were added to the NBA—Buffalo, Cleveland, and Portland. And a trade was completed that changed the power balance in the league. Oscar Robertson was picked up by Milwaukee. Teaming him with Abdul-Jabbar gave the Bucks a powerful one-two punch—one of the greatest of all time—and transformed the Bucks overnight into a terrific team.

Going into the season, the Knicks were largely intact and everybody was optimistic about our stacking up back-to-back championships. We had the personnel, but I knew we also needed the breaks. It was a tough league with a lot of new talent out there.

Walt Frazier came into his own that season. Fourth in the NBA in assists, he also had a 21.7 scoring average. Clyde quarterbacked the Knicks—stealing balls, making great passes, penetrating for his shot. Everything he did seemed so effortless, so smooth, so cool. He's probably the most controlled and collected player I ever coached.

Bradley's stats that season—all those seasons—never showed his true value. He only averaged 12.4 points a game in 1970–71, but what he contributed can never be measured in numbers. I had always stressed ball movement, and Bill was a fanatic on the subject.

"Move the damn ball, move the damn ball!" I can still hear Bill screaming those words as our guys worked to hit the open man for the best percentage shots.

We wound up the year with a 52–30 record and a .630 percentage, second best in the NBA to Milwaukee. The Bucks with Oscar Robertson and Kareem Abdul-Jabbar were 66–16 for an .805 winning percentage, and their shooting percentage was an incredible 50.9. We led the league in defensive average—fewest points allowed—for the third year in a row and finished first in the Atlantic Division five games ahead of Philadelphia. We had 25 sellouts and drew 763,487 to the Garden—the highest home attendance in Knick history to that point.

There was a new playoff system that year since the league had been split into four divisions: Atlantic and Central in the Eastern Conference, and Midwest and Pacific in the Western Conference. In the new arrangement the first-place team in one division played the second-place club in the other division in its conference.

We played Atlanta and defeated them in five games in the first round of the playoffs. In the semifinals we matched up against Baltimore. They had been the only team in the weak Central Division with a record over .500—and they were only two games over. We had beaten Baltimore in four of six games played during the season. However, when you get down to one series, to one game, it doesn't matter what your record was or what their record was.

We won the first two games, and the Bullets beat us pretty badly the next two games. Back in New York we just about beat them. Our offense was sputtering. In games three, four, and five we scored just 88, 80, and 84 points. They took us apart in Baltimore in the sixth game 113–96. We were struggling.

The series came down to the final seconds of the final game. Down by two points, we ran a play for Bill Bradley but somehow burly Wes Unseld fought through the screen. He got a little piece of the ball as Bradley put it up and that was the end of that. We lost 93–91. It was a big disappointment to lose to the Bullets since we had handled them pretty well all year and felt we had a good enough team to go on and win it all.

The good news was that that loss to the Bullets set the stage for two major deals that enabled me to restructure the Knicks. Earl Monroe was deadly in that series, just tremendous. Then we heard that he was unhappy in Baltimore and wanted to leave and go play for a big-city team like the Knicks or L.A. I kept my eye on that situation, figuring it would be to our advantage to get a player of his ability, especially since Dick Barnett was getting a little older (although in 1970–71 he had played in every game for the third straight year).

I also realized Willis would need a year off. At the end of the season he had some physical problems and missed several games. And I started to look around for a quality center. Bob Ferrick, general manager of the San Francisco Warriors, whom I had played basketball with in the Navy, was looking to move Jerry Lucas. He wanted a player like Cazzie Russell.

I had to do what I thought was best for the team. Although Cazzie was extremely popular in New York—and with me—when the season ended I made the deal.

Cazzie Russell had starred in basketball at Carver High School on the south side of Chicago. He always gave the custodial staff there credit for helping his development. They would turn the lights on in the gym and let him practice there all night long. "If it weren't for them letting me practice," he told me, "I might have wound up driving a cab or working in the steel mill or pushing rocks on a construction gang."

Caz moved on from Carver High to play his college ball at

Michigan. In his senior year he averaged almost 31 points a game—
one third of his team's average—and was voted the Player of the Year
in college basketball.

We selected him in the first round in the 1966 draft. Arthur Morse,
his agent, got him a hell of a contract with the Knicks. That deal was
one of the first big-money contracts in pro basketball. With salary and
bonuses it came to $200,000 for three years. That may be small change
by today's standards, but it was big bucks at the time. And it put
pressure on Caz to prove to the other players, the fans, and the media
that he was worth all that money. Cazzie proved he was deserving. He
was an outstanding player, and he brought a lot of excitement to the
Knick game.

Likable and loquacious (I think that means fond of talking), Cazzie
had a great voice and put it to all kinds of uses. He did perfect
impersonations of sports announcers and loved being a mimic.
Midnight Cowboy was a hit movie at that time. And when Dustin
Hoffman came to our games, Cazzie would mimic the way Dustin
walked and talked in the film. And sometimes Dustin would imitate
Cazzie imitating him.

All the time Cazzie was on the Knicks he would complain that he
wanted to be in the starting lineup. I never held that against him
because his bitching showed he had a healthy attitude and confidence
in his ability. In my team scheme of things it worked better to have Bill
Bradley start instead of Cazzie. Bill was not that effective coming off
the bench. Caz was perfectly suited to that role. He was an explosive
scorer who gave us instant offense.

Cazzie always took care of his body and spent a lot of time jumping
rope and working out. He was a superb physical specimen. The credit
for introducing health foods into the NBA probably belongs to him.
Cazzie was into wheat germ, alfalfa sprouts, tiger's milk—all kinds of
appetizing stuff like that.

One day Cazzie was relaxing by his locker after a hard workout. A
reporter came over and while they got to talking Cazzie took out a little
tea set that he always carried around with him and plugged the teapot
into the wall outlet. Soon Caz was sipping tea like an English
gentleman.

The reporter was intrigued. "How come you drink that stuff?" he
asked Cazzie.

"It calms your nerves," Cazzie began. "And what's more," Cazzie continued, "the medicinal value is highly beneficial."

Then Cazzie went on like a medical professor, lecturing the reporter on vitamins and health foods. He opened the top of his locker and showed the reporter all kinds of stuff, most of it samples he had gotten for nothing.

"These things"—there was a very serious tone to Cazzie's voice—"are health-blessed and they are natural." Then he gave the reporter a couple of packages. "You try these and you will be a new man."

The next day we were all boarding the bus for a trip to a game in Philadelphia. Danny Whelan always packed sandwiches for the players and would give them out as the guys came on the bus.

Cazzie entered the bus and Danny asked: "What kind of sandwich would you like?"

"I'll have a bologna on white."

That was Cazzie Russell. He was seriously into health foods, vitamins, and good eating, but he ate what we all ate when he had to.

My fondest memory of Cazzie dates back to May 1971. One Sunday morning soon after the season ended, Selma and I got out early and headed to a father-son church breakfast in Queens where I had agreed to give a speech. Selma came along as my navigator because of my poor sense of direction. I had also prevailed on, some would say leaned on, Dick Barnett to meet us at the breakfast and also give a little talk.

"Hey, Red," I remember Dick telling me, "you ain't gonna show. That's why you want me there."

Unfortunately, Dick was right. Our car skidded in the rain and we hit another car head on. My car was totaled and for a few moments I thought Selma and I were too. We wound up in St. Joseph's Hospital in Far Rockaway.

We were placed in adjoining rooms. Selma's hip was smashed and she was hospitalized for three months. My head was bashed in, swollen to the size of a basketball, and I also had a bunch of broken ribs.

You never really know what people think of you until trouble comes along. That time in the hospital showed how many friends we had. Flowers and cards piled up in both our rooms.

Knick players came to visit us and they created a stir in the hospital since they were such big people. Perhaps the most memorable visitor was Cazzie Russell. I had traded him away just two weeks before. Yet he came in to cheer Selma up, and he brought her an azalea plant. It might sound corny but that visit did a lot for my wife, who was in pain. It showed what kind of guy Cazzie was.

Selma and I later planted the azalea bush in our backyard, and it's still thriving there—a reminder of Cazzie Russell and his fine character.

We gave up a good player and a good man in Cazzie Russell to get Jerry Lucas, who was considered by many to be the greatest basketball player to ever come out of Ohio. His Middletown High School team won 76 straight games and two state championships. Jerry scored 2,466 points as a schoolboy—20 more than Wilt Chamberlain's high school record. From 1959 to 1962 Luke led all college scorers in field goal accuracy. Ohio State had a 78–6 record and three Big Ten championships. The Buckeyes, with Lucas leading the way, were in the finals of the NCAA twice—winning once and losing to Cincinnati the other time.

I had watched Lucas play in college. He was a tremendous center and could hook with either hand, hit jumpers, use his great touch on tip-ins and his intelligence to pass off to a player cutting to the basket. And even though he had been used as a power forward in the NBA till then, I knew he would be a tremendous center for us. I also knew that since we had ranked only 15th in rebounding the year before, Luke would be a big help on the boards. In 1969–70, playing for the Warriors, Jerry was fifth in rebounding in the league.

Lucas was hungry to win, having played seven years in the NBA before we traded for him with little to show for it. We expected a lot from him, and he turned out to be even better than we hoped. Some people gave me credit for making him better. I don't know about that, but I sure didn't make him any worse. He was very bright, a great team player, and he fit in perfectly with what we were attempting to do.

A handsome guy, a piece of cake to handle, Jerry was never a problem for me and he added a special spirit to the team.

Jerry was always looking around for something to do. He would memorize the phone book, newspapers, anything to keep himself occupied.

Poker games where money is shown were not allowed on planes and in some other places. If the players couldn't use money, they used Jerry. He could keep records in his head of what everybody won and lost on each pot, what everybody owed. They'd be playing for hours and he'd be sitting there reading a book. When they finished playing, Jerry would report the results. All the guys accepted that as gospel because Jerry never made any mistakes.

I would tell Jerry that his mind was full of all kinds of crap and could memorize anything but that he didn't remember one single play that we used. Of course it was a joke—Luke knew all the plays. He even knew what all the statistics were for the team at the end of a game—before they were printed out on the stat sheet.

He was a guy with the gift of gab who could distract anybody, which contributed to his skill as a magician. Lucas always carried props around with him—coins, charms, trick cards—a grab bag of stuff.

The Jerry Lucas–Cazzie Russell deal was easy to make. It was a straight swap. San Francisco wanted Cazzie, and I was convinced that Luke would fit in perfectly with us.

The deal for Earl Monroe was much tougher, and I had to jockey back and forth with Baltimore throughout the summer of 1971. The deal was on and off, off and on.

Finally on November 10, 1971, we acquired the Pearl, giving up Mike Riordan, Dave Stallworth, and cash. It was a lot to give up, but for a player like Earl you had to give a lot.

There was some criticism of the trade. Some said that we'd need two basketballs with Earl Monroe and Walt Frazier on the same team. Others said that Earl was sure to come in with his individualistic style and disrupt things. I didn't buy any of that.

I had first seen Earl Monroe playing for Coach Bighouse Gaines at Winston-Salem College. He was an all-around kind of player there, even though when he got to the NBA with Baltimore, his game switched to one-to-one. I knew what Earl's potential was, and I was confident that my coaching and belief in team offense and defense would help Earl's game.

At Baltimore, Earl had played on winning teams, but they had never won a championship. He was happy to come to New York City. Since he had to adjust to the role of our third guard in 1971–72 behind Dick Barnett and Walt Frazier, and since he was recovering from an off-season operation for a bone spur, Earl had some troubles fitting in at first. He averaged just 11.9 points a game that season, but it didn't matter to me. A player figured to score less in our system than he would with other teams. I was happy with Earl's progress and the way he learned our team defense and offensive discipline.

On the court Earl was a master showman, the most flamboyant player I ever coached. He could easily have played for the Harlem Globetrotters. Off the court, the Pearl was quiet, shy, liked by everybody, and very helpful to the younger players.

Earl had a remarkable ability to control his body. Although it looked like he was taking off-balance shots, the Pearl was never off balance. He was always under great control. Earl was a very, very smart basketball player, but many fans and players didn't realize this. That worked to his advantage, and he was able to do things no one expected him to.

Using his great head fakes and body feints, Earl would get you in the air, get you in a leaning position, get you so that no matter how big you were, there was no way you could block his shot. He possessed all the tools, and he also had that great, great touch.

Earl had an uncanny knack of scoring from anyplace on the floor, using the most unorthodox shots. One night we had a game won, and Earl was down in the corner with the ball, with a few seconds left in the game. Wanting the clock to run out, he heaved a hook shot at the other team's basket. The shot went in. Although Earl was just kidding around, there was an investigation because his shot had affected the gambling point spread.

Earl Monroe was a gentle man, but he also played with a great deal of pride, which sometimes got him into trouble with the refs. One night he was thrown out of a game for talking back too much. The next night he came out for the warmup drill with a piece of tape over his mouth. The referees could have thrown him out again, but we told them that Earl had a cut lip.

Nicknamed "The Ghost" by the players, Earl would cut things really close, like not arriving for the team bus or a plane trip and then suddenly materializing at the last second. Even off the court he had a magic touch about being where he was supposed to be and having things work out to his advantage.

We were at Kennedy Airport one night, waiting for our plane to take off. Earl hadn't shown up. The flight was cancelled and we were shifted to LaGuardia Airport. When we arrived at LaGuardia, Earl was already there. He had made a mistake and gone to the wrong airport, but even the mistake worked in his favor.

In addition to restructuring the Knicks in 1971–72 with a once-in-a-lifetime player like Earl Monroe and a great player like Jerry Lucas, we also added Dean "The Dream" Meminger from Marquette. Dean had been scouted by Dick McGuire and coached by his brother, Al McGuire. As a rookie, Dean played 1,173 minutes, all quality time. Not a great shooter, Dean made up for that with his fine defense—he was able to come into a game and shut down high scoring guards.

Intense, a hyper type of guy, Meminger had a short upper body and very long legs. If he had had the torso to match the length of his legs, he would have measured about six foot nine.

Dean added a lot of spirit to the team and always wanted the guys to play all out. If he caught them letting down, he'd jump all over them, and he was just a rookie. There was a good chemistry on the court between him and Jerry Lucas, and they ran a few special plays very well off the pivot.

The final standings for 1971–72 showed that the power in the league had shifted to the Midwest and Pacific Division. L.A. had a 69–13 record, and had won its division by 18 games. Lew Alcindor, who changed his name that year to Kareem Abdul-Jabbar, won the scoring title with a 34.8 average, and Milwaukee posted a 63–19 record in the Midwest Division. Baltimore won in the Central, where every team lost more games than they won. We finished with a 48–34 mark, eight games behind Boston, winner of its first division title in seven years. They had Jo Jo White, John Havlicek, Don Nelson, Dave Cowens, and a deep, deep bench.

It was a good thing that we had made the trade for Lucas, since Willis Reed played in only 11 games. Luke was invaluable, averaging almost 17 points a game and pulling down almost a thousand rebounds—and he wasn't that big or that good a jumper. What helped him, however, was that he knew how to get in position to get the rebound and make the good outlet pass. He was one of the greatest passers off the center spot that I've ever seen. His 318 assists that season placed him second only to Walt Frazier. Quite an accomplishment for a center.

Luke was perfect for us, a great shooter with long range. He'd get out there and they'd have to come out and play him or he'd hit the outside shot all night. If Luke were playing today, he'd probably lead the league in three-point shots. His outside play as a center opened up the middle for our team and gave us many options on offense.

We beat Baltimore 4–1 and Boston 4–1 and then matched up against Los Angeles in the championship series. Considering we were playing without Willis, we did very well to get to that point.

In the first game against the Lakers I designed a special pick and roll with Lucas and Bradley. Wilt Chamberlain was hesitant about coming out to guard Luke, and we exploited that. The maneuver paid off, and we crushed L.A. by 22 points. Many of the 17,505 fans at the Forum were so demoralized that they got up and walked out midway through the second half.

We were leading in the second game when DeBusschere injured his hip. With a crippled DeBusschere and no Willis Reed we had too many handicaps. L.A. swept the rest of the series. If Dave had not gotten hurt, we could have had a 2–0 lead and probably would have won the championship. But it was their turn.

CHAPTER 4

Willis Reed had missed almost all of the 1971–72 season because of knee surgery. He was ready to stage a comeback, and I was determined to do all I could to help him get his confidence back as we started thinking about the new season. I realized Willis was going to be 30 years old when the 1972–73 season began, and that his body had taken a lot of pounding in his time with the Knicks. That was one of the reasons we went for size in the NBA draft.

We picked Tom Riker, six foot ten, of South Carolina in the first round, although we were wavering between Tom and John Gianelli, another six-ten prospect, who was drafted by Houston in the second round. We wound up with both of them when we purchased Gianelli from Houston. It meant more size and more insurance against a mistake. We drafted Henry Bibby of UCLA in the fourth round. He was a little guy, just a little over six feet tall, but he was a winning player.

In training camp Gianelli showed a lot of talent. He played so well blocking shots and running that we thought we had the next Bill Russell. John was Italian, but he didn't act like he knew he was. I thought he'd know some good places to go for Italian food or at least a way to get access to some good home-cooked stuff. But as an eater, John disappointed me.

Bibby was the best player at getting things done in a training camp that I ever saw in all my years as a scout or a coach. He was letter-perfect. He didn't let down in a drill for a second. He never dogged it. Henry was the first UCLA player I coached, and although I always had a lot of respect for Coach John Wooden's program, seeing a product of that program like Bibby made me admire the UCLA system even more. There was no way to keep Henry Bibby off the Knicks despite his small size. Relentless in everything he did, there was no limit to his desire to please or to his knowledge of the game.

Tom Riker was another story. Both he and John Gianelli were represented by Arthur Morse, the lawyer who had represented Cazzie Russell. I always had a lot of respect for Morse, who took good care of his players, but Riker didn't take the same good care of himself. He liked to eat too much and showed up for training camp overweight and out of shape.

The surprise of the 1972–73 training camp was six-foot-eight Harthorne Wingo who had played basketball for just one year at Freedom Junior College in his home state of North Carolina. He had grown up there as one of fourteen kids—seven brothers and seven sisters in a very poor family.

Wingo was a walk-on. He came to the Knicks after Dave Stallworth spotted him playing in the Rucker Tournament in Harlem. Dave told me about Wingo, so I sent Dick McGuire and Dick Barnett to look him over. They liked what they saw and we told him to report to training camp. It was then that I learned Wingo supported himself in New York City by pushing a hand truck in the garment center.

"You know, Wingo," I told him, "I once hand-trucked it too."

"Coach," he smiled, "you must have done it for a gag." Whether he ever believed me or not, I always thought the time both of us spent pushing hand trucks in the garment center didn't hurt us a bit.

Wingo had big hands and at six eight was a great leaper, a true playground player. Even though he didn't have much formal basketball training, he could pass and shoot the ball.

"Growing up in Tryon, North Carolina," Wingo explained to me, "we had to play on dirt courts, where you couldn't dribble the ball too well. And one of the baskets was too high and the other was too low. So we had to work on our shooting and passing to make up for the uneven baskets and the dirt floor."

Wingo had great heart and drive, but unfortunately he didn't survive the training camp that season. "You're not quite ready for the NBA," I said. "You go to Allentown in the Eastern League. Do well there and stay by the phone. Stay ready. I promise I'm gonna call you."

My sixth season as coach of the New York Knickerbockers began in 1972–73. My personal routines were pretty well established, and everyone knew what to expect.

On the road I had things worked out to make the most out of being away from Selma's home cooking. There was a rumor that I judged a city by two things: its racetrack facilities and its restaurants, and there was a lot of truth to that rumor.

When we arrived in a city the day before the game, I would make it a practice to visit any racetrack that was nearby. It was a great form of relaxation. On West Coast trips we'd go to the track in the afternoon. When we played in Detroit I'd cross the border into Canada and patronize Windsor, a harness racing track, one of my favorite places to bet a couple of dollars.

Before a game I never ate much—I functioned better that way—hungry. After a game was over, however, I made up for the lost calories. I would get together with my guys, trainer Danny Whelan, publicity man Frankie Blauschild, and some of the New York press.

Our routine consisted of a waiting period, usually in Danny's room, until all the guys finished writing their stories or whatever work they had to do. Some might have called that waiting period a cocktail hour. When everyone finally assembled, we'd pile into rental cars and head out to a good restaurant.

Real dining began after midnight, when the game would be rehashed while the food was digested. I picked up a lot of tips about eating in restaurants during those adventures. I learned never to make small talk with a waiter or waitress or kid around too much before the food was ordered. It slowed down the service, and you might say something they didn't like and you could wind up with problems with your food. I also made it a practice never to take seriously any medical advice given by a waiter. And I learned never to raise my hand to make a point in a restaurant or wave to anybody when the check was coming.

If restaurants were closed by the time we were ready to use them, we'd picnic in Danny's room. In addition to being the world's number one trainer, Danny Whelan possessed a special talent for bringing back buckets of chicken, stone crabs, spare ribs, or other delicacies. Those picnics were almost as much fun as dining out, and all those times were good ways to kill the clock, have some fun, and relieve the relentless pressure of the games.

My routines with the players were pretty set too. I treated them as men. I never posted curfews. I wasn't going to look in on them and see if they were in their room and sleeping. "Just don't fall asleep on the top sheet and catch a cold," I told them.

I think they liked the freedom I gave them, and they didn't abuse it. Maybe half the fun is being able to fool somebody. If there's no curfew, what the hell's the sense of staying out late?

"Stay out of the hotel bar on the road," I told them. "That's where I go and that belongs to me. I'm depending on you guys to take care of yourselves. Go to bed when you need to go to bed. Make sure you get your rest, because if you don't, I'll know it when you're on the court."

That approach seemed to work. In coaching, your ears are a big factor but your eyes are even more important. I developed the ability to look into a player's eyes to detect if he was fired up or tired, into the game or dreaming. If he wasn't able to play, I'd substitute somebody else for him. Back then, the threat of taking playing time away gave coaches control over a player's pride and his pocketbook. A guy playing less was doing less for the team. Another player started to cut into that guy's time, which affected his pride and, ultimately, his paycheck. Today it's a little different with guaranteed contracts cutting somewhat into the power of the coach. Still, the biggest hold a coach has over the player is the reduction of playing time.

All through those years I made my players see that I wasn't going to take any bullshit from them, and that I expected them to conduct themselves like pros and work as hard as I was prepared to work.

Things were a little different back then, but the players bought my approach and worked together as a team.

In those days I never had an assistant coach. I always allowed all the guys to have a say. I realized that if some guy gave me a suggestion, he would bust his ass to make it work. There were times, too, when I had guys on the floor whose combined experience was 20, 25 years in the league. They had to know something, so suggestions were always in order.

Around that time in the early 1970s, other coaches were getting involved with visual aids—charts, schematics on clipboards, little blackboards, diagrams. I never used anything because I wanted to be unencumbered. I never even had a program in my hands when I was coaching. I felt that if I had something handy, I'd throw it and get into trouble.

Another part of my routine was to leave an open seat on each side of me on the bench. I didn't have that many suits in those days and players were wet and sweaty coming off the court, and I wanted to preserve my clothes. The main reason for the open seats, however, was to have some space as a landing zone for players who I wanted to talk to or who wanted to talk to me. When they sat down next to me, I could give them an instant critique or bawl the shit out of them as the situation demanded. Sometimes players gave me information on something happening on the floor that enabled me to make some coaching adjustments.

Although I always cooperated with the press and always tried to be available for an interview, I never allowed cameras or mikes into our huddles. It wasn't an arbitrary thing with me—I had my reasons.

Early in my coaching career in St. Louis I had once allowed the guys with the mikes and the cameras to enter our dressing room. We were getting the hell beat out of us in that game, and I had wanted to do some yelling at the players during halftime. It was impossible. My players were sitting there like ten Little Lord Fauntleroys, like nice little boys. They acted like they hadn't committed any screwups at all during the first half. Didn't even know what a screwup *was*. With the media in there I felt I was no longer a coach, but more like a guy in the role of a TV actor. How could I get mad at any of my players in that situation? How could I jump on them or use any profanity? All I could do was fume—quietly and politely.

That experience taught me to ban electronic media from huddles. I always recognized my responsibility to the media, but my main responsibility was to the team. I wasn't afraid of giving away any trade secrets, but it was distracting and inhibiting to have cameras and mikes there.

I also saw some coaches get hurt by allowing cameras and mikes in the huddles. They would make up a play and it would backfire, or they would be talking to a player and the guy would be looking at some woman in the stands. Other coaches handled the electronic media on the bench or in the huddle very well. For me, it was not my thing—I was dedicated one thousand percent to coaching and I didn't want any interference or distractions.

I also had worked out a way to handle autographs. A very humbling experience taught me how to do it efficiently. We were playing on the road and a bunch of kids cornered me for my autograph. I had them form a nice, straight line. The first kid gave me a piece of paper and I was about to sign my name when someone yelled: "Hey, there's Walt Frazier!"

The kid who had just given me the piece of paper to sign yanked it out of my hand and went running with the other kids after Walt. That was demoralizing, but I always tried to learn something from defeat.

After that experience, anytime I was in a hurry and a bunch of kids cornered me for my autograph I'd yell, "Hey, there's Walt Frazier!" The kids would take off, and I'd be on my way too.

To this day I'm actually very happy to sign autographs. I always did much better when I was signing them than when I wasn't signing them. When they don't ask for your autograph, then you know there's a problem. I still sign autographs anytime, anyplace, as long as people don't get abusive.

The funniest autograph experiences are always with kids. "Who do you think I am?" I ask them.

"You used to be the coach of the Knicks," they answer.

"What's the coach of the Knicks mean?" I ask them.

"I don't know . . ." is usually the answer.

"What are you going to do with the autograph when you get home?"

"I'm going to keep it" is another standard answer.

"How long are you going to keep it?"

"I don't know" is a typically truthful response.

Sometimes I think kids collect ten Red Holzman autographs so they can trade them for one Bernard King signature. But kids are refreshing, and I have always loved to talk to them.

Their fathers, though, can sometimes get on your nerves, especially when they give you the line: "Hey, buddy, didn't you used to be Red Holzman?"

As we moved into the 1972–73 season we were three deep at the center position with Reed, Lucas, and Gianelli, plus Phil Jackson was also available to fill in there. Monroe and Frazier would handle most of the playing time at the guard position backed by Meminger, Bibby, and Barnett. I planned to have Bradley and DeBusschere play as much as possible at the forward spots and Phil Jackson and Jerry Lucas were there to back them up. We had a lot of depth, a lot of defense, and I pegged my coaching tactics around those strengths.

Early that season, on November 18, 1972, the greatest comeback I was ever involved in as a player or a coach took place at Madison Square Garden. It was a game against the Milwaukee Bucks that would become a symbol of my philosophy, my experience, my time in the game—all the things I had worked so hard to teach our players. The thrill of it all was overcoming what seemed impossible odds.

We came into the game with a 15–3 record while Milwaukee had won 12 of its first 16 games. They had a great shooting team, with Bobby Dandridge, John McGlocklin, Lucius Allen, Oscar Robertson, and Kareem Abdul-Jabbar in his third season as a pro. Jabbar always seemed to try a little harder against us. Maybe it was because he had grown up in New York City and wanted to make a good showing against us in his hometown. Maybe it was because our fans weren't too kind to him when he made a mistake.

In one game early in his career they really got on his case. The whole Garden broke into song, singing a dozen choruses of "Goodbye, Looie" to the tune "Good-night, Ladies." (He was known as Lew Alcindor then.) Even some of our players felt a little sorry for him after that razzing.

Nobody razzed Jabbar in the game on November 18, 1972. With 5:50 left to play, we were being crushed. We were down by 18 points,

86–68. On defense Jabbar was all arms and legs. He was relentless on offense with 32 points, playing as if it were a grudge match.

Things didn't look good, but I wasn't rattled, knowing from experience that anything could happen in basketball. Besides, I wasn't going anyplace anyway. I knew if we kept the pressure on the Bucks and got some breaks, we would have a chance. We had won other games that year with last-minute rallies and would win a lot more coming back from what looked like knockouts. That was a special thing about my teams then. Like thoroughbreds, they had the capacity to rise to the occasion no matter what other teams did. They always had the ability and the heart to come back. I called time and in the huddle thought to myself that all we had to do was score 19 points and hold the Bucks scoreless and we would be able to win.

It was wishful thinking, but not crazy. In pro basketball almost five minutes to play in a game is a lifetime. With the 24-second clock operating and with the clock dead on everything in the last two minutes, anything is possible: steals, three-point plays, five-point turnarounds in a few seconds. That was another way the game had changed a great deal from the early days.

At 4:52 Earl Monroe made a driving lay-up and was fouled. Earl's free throw cut the lead to 15 points, 86–71. Eddie Layton at the Garden organ played a little louder and the fans were yelling "Dee-fense, dee-fense!" Dandridge made a bad pass, and Frazier took advantage of the turnover, cutting in for a driving lay-up. Milwaukee's lead was sliced to 13 points. The Bucks called a time-out and attempted to regroup. The noise level at the Garden was incredible.

With four minutes and 12 seconds left, Frazier hit from the corner, making the score 86–75. Pandemonium ruled at the Garden—some people were standing on their seats.

Robertson and Jabbar both missed shots, and Monroe hit from the baseline, making the score 86–77. The momentum was swinging to our side. Robertson fumbled the ball, and Monroe canned one from the outside at the 3:13 mark. We were within seven points of catching them.

Jabbar missed a hook shot. DeBusschere scored. We trailed by five. With 2:20 left, Milwaukee head coach Larry Costello called time to try to settle his team down. At this point the Garden was really rocking—the fans were on their feet applauding us.

Play resumed. Dandridge missed his shot, rebounded, shot again. Missed. Monroe broke ahead of the field and drove in for a lay-up. We trailed by just three points and the Garden was bedlam. Jabbar and Robertson both missed shots. With 47 seconds left, Frazier was at the line to shoot two foul shots. Clyde was unflappable. He calmly dropped both in. It was a one-point game.

Robertson took the ball out for the Bucks at midcourt. Earl Monroe fouled Allen, and he missed both foul shot attempts. Willis rebounded. We went on offense, and the building actually shook as Monroe sank a jumper from the key with 36 seconds left. We led by one point.

Jabbar missed a hook shot with 27 seconds left. DeBusschere rebounded the missed shot and passed the ball to Bradley, who held the ball. The 24-second clock ran out on us, and they got the ball back with one second left in the game. Their last shot kind of symbolized what happened to them as Jabbar took a long hook from along the baseline. He missed. The final score stood at 87–86.

We had scored the last 19 points in the game and pitched a shutout at the Bucks at the same time. It seemed like an impossible accomplishment, and we had some breaks along the way. But it was our system that had made it possible for our players to operate almost instinctively. We played as a team, and we won as a team. It was our discipline, our unselfishness, and our confidence in our ability that won it for us.

We finished the 1972–73 season in second place in the Atlantic Division with a 57–25 record, 11 games behind the Boston Celtics. They were 68–14 and had won more games than any other team in the NBA that year. Baltimore (who had changed its name to Capitol), Milwaukee, and Los Angeles won in the other divisions.

I was pretty satisfied with the way things had worked out, especially my rotating Reed and Lucas. Willis averaged 11 points a game and Jerry averaged close to 10 points, so we managed 20 points out of the center position. We also allowed just 98.2 points a game on defense—the lowest average of any team I ever coached.

Once again the Bullets were our opponent as we entered the playoffs. We defeated them 102–91 in the opener at the Garden and went on to take the series four games to one.

RED ON RED   137

Next we met the Boston Celtics, in the Eastern Conference finals. They had a powerful team. John Havlicek, their sixth man coming off the bench, was team-minded and had great drive. It's easy to talk about "Hondo," and yet it's hard to say something about him that hasn't been said. He was simply one of the greatest players I ever saw.

Havlicek and Dave Cowens had both averaged more than 20 points a game during the regular season and were fierce players. Boston also had Jo Jo White, Paul Silas, Don Chaney, and a bench that went very deep.

The coach of the Celtics was Tom Heinsohn, whose image was that of a big, rough guy, a screamer. He was big all right, but the rest was for show. Tommy was sensitive and intelligent. He was also a painter and had a successful insurance business. He was a great coach who prepared his team very well. Despite the intensity of the Celtics–Knicks rivalry, Tommy and I always had a friendly relationship.

Boston Garden is an old arena with tons of atmosphere. It's a great place to play basketball. With all those pennants hanging there, the surroundings can pump you up or intimidate you, depending on what kind of players you have. Their fans were always a little more than partial to the home team and antagonistic to the visiting team, but they were great fans. We never resented the screaming.

A lot of the Celtic fan jibes directed at us were triggered by New York writers claiming the Knicks were going to be the next NBA dynasty to replace Boston. After we won in 1969–70 and didn't win the next year, Boston fans would scream: "Hey, where's the dynasty?" They had a lot of fun with that.

If you could go in and win in Boston Garden, that was a real accomplishment, because with their crowd behind them and their proud tradition, the Celtics were especially tough. A great deal of the credit for what Boston accomplished has to go to Red Auerbach, who coached them from 1950–66. Owners came and went, but all of them allowed him to do his thing, run the Celtics his way.

The Eastern Conference finals against Boston got under way on April 15, 1972, at Boston Garden. We were given an old beat-up dressing room; they wouldn't let us use their whirlpool. It was psychological warfare, the Celtic fun-and-games version, but I wasn't too unhappy about it. I realized there could be an advantage to our disadvantage there. It was a little bit like our situation with Baltimore in 1968–69, when the Bullets said they wanted us in the playoffs and Walt Frazier coined the slogan "They chose us."

Now Walt went around bitching about the way the Celtics were treating us, and I didn't discourage him. He kept telling our guys that Boston didn't respect us. "Teach them respect!" became the Knicks' new slogan. We had a little trouble getting that to work in the first game as the Celtics crushed us 134–108.

In the second game, played in New York, the crowd was ready and so were we. "Dee-fense, dee-fense, dee-fense!" That word roared from more than 19,500 throats hundreds of times throughout the game. Dean Meminger did a tremendous job of holding down Jo Jo White, and we kept the Celts under a hundred points to win the game 129–96.

We traveled back to Boston for the third game. This time we were given a different dressing room. It was even worse than the one we had for the first game, smaller, more out of the way, really cramped.

"It's a pain being switched from place to place," Phil Jackson bitched.

"This dressing room is for jockeys, not basketball players," said Walt Frazier.

"We'll make the best of it, guys," I told them. "Take it out on the Celtics on the floor."

We did. We won that third game 98–91. And then we pulled out an OT win in the fourth game at Madison Square Garden.

Back in Boston for the fifth game, we were given a different dressing room once again. This one was dusty *and* dirty. It was like a sauna—the temperature must have been about 120 degrees.

Phil Jackson fumed. Willis Reed grumbled. And Walt Frazier kept repeating, "Teach the Celtics respect. They don't respect us." Dick Barnett added: "Way to go, Clyde."

That fifth game was a furious defensive battle as the Celtic fans went wild, cheering their team on to a narrow 98–97 win. That set up the sixth game back at Madison Square Garden. All we had to do was to win that game on our home floor and we would move into the final round of the playoffs. To Boston's credit they didn't fold. They beat us 110–100, setting up the seventh game in Boston.

I thought we had taken an awful screwing from the referees in the sixth game, and I was worried about the seventh game in Boston, which was a tough, tough place for us to play.

A few minutes before the seventh game got under way, I spotted John Nucatola, the head of the NBA officials, under the stands. I cornered him.

"John," I started easy. "We got an awful screwing in the game in New York. I don't want the refs harboring any old feelings in this game. I'm not asking for any special treatment, but you gotta have your guys stand up to the Boston fans. The home court edge here is tremendous, and I don't want that to sway them."

John didn't say much but kept shaking his head as if he were trying to pacify me. That only made me angrier. Finally I resorted to using some strong language. Part of it was an act, but I was determined to get him to raise his refs' consciousness.

Usually, my tactic was to gently needle the refs. I'd give them lines like "You're a better official than that" or "I can't believe you made that call." Coaching in that seventh game, I was anything but gentle. I was riding the refs throughout the game. Usually at Boston they throw you out for making a fuss, but I was able to get away with murder and felt pretty good about it, thinking that my passionate plea to John Nucatola who I'd always liked and respected had been good for something. It wasn't until later, however, that I learned that John has poor hearing and there's a good possibility that he never heard a damned word I said. If he did, he would have probably thrown me out of Boston Garden.

My encounter with John Nucatola wasn't really necessary. Our defense was tremendous, and we slaughtered Boston 94–78. It was one of the most satisfying wins of my career and put the Knicks into the NBA finals for the third time in four years.

The Los Angeles Lakers were our competition in the finals once again. And once again they were an imposing team, with Jerry West, Wilt Chamberlain, Gail Goodrich, Jim McMillian, Happy Hairston, and a young utility player named Pat Riley. L.A. had finished the year with a 60–22 record and defeated Chicago and Golden State in the playoffs.

There was a little bit of bad blood between our guys and the Lakers because the newspapers had reported them saying they wanted us in the finals, not the Celtics. Frazier was usually pretty quiet but on the chartered jet out to L.A. for the first game he kept saying, "They wanted us. They got us. Let's give them something to remember." I didn't encourage Walt or discourage him. I felt pretty good about our chances after the Boston series. The team had a lot of intensity; we were at our peak.

One of the happiest of all our players was Harthorne Wingo, who had played in 13 games after we recalled him from Allentown during the season. I think it was the first time in his life he had ever been to California.

The Lakers nipped us 115–112 in the first game. We reviewed film more than any other team in the NBA at the time, and studying that game's film I noted how much the Laker game plan hinged on how and where Chamberlain set up. I made some defensive changes, and we swept the next four games, holding the Lakers to under 100 points in each of them. We were the NBA champions!

Wilt Chamberlain's statement to the press summed up some of what had happened. "The Knicks are so well balanced and have tremendous passing and so many good shooters that you can't concentrate on one man. The key to the series was that their defense stopped our running game."

Not since the Boston dynasty ended in 1969 had an NBA team repeated as champions, until the Knicks. I felt pretty good about that. Making the NBA finals three out of four years and winning the title twice was something no other team had accomplished during that period. I felt pretty good about that too.

Flying back on the plane from Los Angeles to New York City was one big party. Jerry Lucas was especially happy. After ten years in the league he had his first NBA championship ring to add to a collection that included high school, NCAA, and Olympics. Henry Bibby kept telling everyone that he was a good luck charm. "This is my fourth championship in a row," he said. Henry had starred on three NCAA championship teams at UCLA.

Willis Reed was selected as the Most Valuable Player in the playoffs, and he was also feeling no pain. "Well, the Lakers wanted us and they sure got us," he said. "They didn't turn their title over to us. We took it. We learned from the Boston series that when you get a team down 3–1, you should kill 'em right away, and that's what we did to L.A.''

More than 1,000 fans were at Kennedy Airport to welcome us back to New York City. "We're number one! We're number one!" Those fans were loyal but they also were a little wild. I was afraid some of our guys would get hurt. Bibby, Meminger, Gianelli, and Frazier bravely made their way through the crowd, even though they were slapped on the back and pawed at. The rest of us slipped out through a back door. An escape route, complete with waiting cars, had been arranged by my daughter, Gail, who at that time was a customs agent at the airport.

A few days later we had a big party at Tavern on the Green in Central Park in Manhattan. All the players were there with their families and friends. Mr. Felt made a long speech and ended it this way:

"If Red Holzman doesn't come to see me tomorrow about changing his contract, then he's not as smart as I think he is.''

Winning that championship was wonderful. There's no feeling quite like it, but the way Mr. Felt acted was icing on the cake. It showed his character, appreciation, and generosity. He really didn't have to make that gesture in public.

By the way, I was in his office the next day.

For years I had felt the first Knick championship team was the best. It was the one the press and the fans seemed to give the most credit. It was my first Knick NBA title team and that group always had a special spot in my heart. Now, looking back at things a little more objectively, I think the 1972–73 team was a little better. It was deeper, more experienced. The first team had Reed and Bowman at the center spot. Reed and Lucas on the 1972–73 team were much stronger. Lucas gave us insurance at two positions, forward and center. He could rebound, pass the ball, and shoot outside. That gave us great versatility. We also had Gianelli as the third center, if needed, and that gave us still greater depth.

At the guards, Frazier and Monroe were backed up three deep. Bibby was a tremendous third guard, and Meminger and Barnett played fourth and fifth guards as needed. Earl really came into his own during that second championship season after adjusting to our team and what we were doing the first year or so.

Bradley and DeBusschere at the forward spots were just perfect together. By 1972–73, they had played together for a while and were in a kind of automatic synch. And Phil Jackson and his hustling ways added still another part to the whole that made that team deep.

The 1969–70 team showcased a new brand of basketball with the ultimate object being team play, passing the ball, sacrificing. It wasn't that big a team, so we had to make adjustments. The 1972–73 team had a little more size, depth, more dimensions.

I was probably a better coach, too, because I had had the experience of working with the same nucleus of players for several seasons. I knew what they could do, and what I could do with them. And because they had more dimension as a team I could do more with them, even though our basic philosophy was still the same.

We looked good winning our second NBA championship. And once again there were those who talked about us beginning a new basketball dynasty that spring of 1973; unfortunately, however, our team was moving into the autumn of its life.

Dick Barnett had not been used much that 1972–73 season. He was 36 years old. Lucas was 33. Willis Reed and Bill Bradley were approaching their 31st and 30th birthdays. DeBusschere would be 33 by the time the new season began. I was already feeling the pressure of sustaining what we had. Injuries, age, and guys who were beginning to think of doing other things with their lives were the reality I had to deal with as coach and general manager.

We tried to make a trade to help the team, but making any kind of significant deal was a problem. Our guys were getting older, and even though their ability was still great, their trade value was not that high. In the 1973 draft we picked fourteenth and made Mel Davis of St. John's University our choice. He never worked out as we thought he should.

Nevertheless, as we began the 1973–74 season, it seemed the team could still have another good year. I thought it was even possible for us to win the whole thing again and then restructure. Unfortunately, we had a lot of bad breaks that season.

Monroe was operated on and missed 41 games. Willis was banged up and played in just 19. Both Bibby and Gianelli were injured and were sub-par.

Considering all these problems, we still had a respectable year. We finished with a 49–33 record, in second place in the Atlantic Division, seven games behind the Celtics. Only four teams won more games than we did, and once again we led the NBA in defensive average. Our offense was down. We averaged just over 101 points a game—third from the bottom in a 17-team league.

The Bullets finished first in the Central Division and were our competition in the playoffs in March 1974. It was the sixth straight year we had come up against them in the playoffs. Only in the 1971 series, when they beat us in the seventh game, had we failed to get by them.

Willis and Earl kidded about the playoffs. "Are you going to have another great series against your old team?" Willis asked the Pearl.

"Nobody left except Unseld." Monroe smiled.

"Take it out on him."

Earl was correct about the Bullets. It was a revamped team with players like Phil Chenier, Elvin Hayes, Kevin Porter, and Archie Clark. And Mike Riordan had become a vital part of that team. In the 1973–74 season he had played 3,230 minutes, almost 40 minutes a game, and averaged almost 16 points a game. Mike had become a tough two-way player. It was a far cry from the days when he had been sent in by me to give a foul and come out. Mike had made himself a great player.

The funny thing about that series was that Mike and Bill Bradley were matched against each other. When they were teammates on the Knicks they had spent many hours playing one-on-one against each other in an empty gym after all the other guys had left. An hour and a half workout was never enough for them.

In our opening game win, the Pearl shot 12 for 17, taking it out first on Archie Clark, then Phil Chenier, then Kevin Porter. He showed them all the old moves and a few new ones. We matched up well against the Bullets and got by them in the first round. Boston was next.

"Ugh," winced Bill Bradley. "First Mike Riordan and now John Havlicek." The Celtics beat us four out of five games and knocked us out of the playoffs. If Willis had been well and Lucas had been up to his game, it might have been a different story, but that's how it was.

When the 1974 playoffs ended, Bill Bradley and Dave De-Busschere, like the rest of us, were exhausted. They decided to get away from all the pressure and attention by heading off to the Greek islands with their wives. They planned to relax and get in some swimming and scuba diving. Typically, all Bill Bradley took along was a small gym bag. He didn't even have a bathing suit—he took along his Knick practice shorts for bathing. Bill always traveled light.

The two couples spent a lot of time lolling about on the deck of their cabin cruiser, soaking up sun. Bill and Dave stirred every so often to put on their flippers and snorkeling masks and check out the fish and shells in the Aegean Sea. One day they spotted a tiny, isolated island with a church on a hill. Bill was curious. "Let's try and get over there," he said to Dave, "and see what it's like."

It was difficult to dock the boat close to the island, so Dave and Bill swam about a quarter of a mile to the shore. The beach was completely deserted except for one man sitting on a beach chair, relaxing and reading a book. DeBusschere—all six foot six of him—plus dripping water and snorkeling mask—came out of the ocean. At that moment the guy looked up. He was so startled that he jumped out of his chair and dropped his book. He must have thought Dave was a creature from Atlantis.

Dave, realizing the guy was shaken up, pulled off his snorkeling mask. With that the guy seemed to go into shock. "DeBusschere. You're Dave DeBusschere," he shouted. "It can't be. I must have gotten too much sun."

At this point Bill Bradley came out of the water and took off his mask. "Everything all right, Dave?" Bill asked.

The guy couldn't believe what he was seeing. He took in Bradley's Knick practice shorts. "Is it really you—DeBusschere and Bradley—or am I dreaming?"

"Sure it's us," Bill joked. "And the rest of the team is coming out of the water in a couple of minutes. We had a tough season and we all came here to Greece for some rest."

"That's why I'm here too," the guy said. "I'm a Knick season ticket holder and I'm exhausted from watching all those games. I came here for some rest too." Then the guy said, "Fellas, stay right where you are. Don't move. I'll be right back. I'm gonna get my wife. She's a big Knick fan too."

The guy took off and so did Dave and Bill, back into the water and onto the boat. Their last glimpse of the island was of two tiny figures. The man was waving wildly and pointing at the footprints Bradley and DeBusschere had left in the sand. And the wife was shaking her head as if she didn't believe a word her husband was saying.

The 1974–75 season was a crossroads for the Knicks because our roster changed in a dramatic way. Three future Hall of Famers quit in one shot: Willis Reed, Jerry Lucas, and Dave DeBusschere all were gone. I always felt the time came for them too soon.

Willis was all banged up with a bad knee that cut his career short. Luke was still in pretty good shape and could have played a little more, but he wanted to get on with his life and pursue his business interests. Of the three, Dave had the most basketball left in him, and could easily have gone on another year or so. Ned Irish and I met with him and tried to persuade Dave to stay. It was not to be. Dave was excited about the opportunity to take over as general manager and vice-president of the New York Nets. Even the argument that he would make more money continuing to play for the Knicks for a couple of years didn't sway DeBusschere. His mind was set on moving on.

Willis, Jerry, and Dave had to do what was best for them. I felt bad, but being a realist, I knew the day would come when I, too, would leave the Knicks. The only constant in basketball is change.

We also lost valuable Dean Meminger to the expansion draft. Only Bradley, Frazier, Monroe, and Jackson remained from the glory years. Dick Barnett stayed on in a new role, as my assistant coach. I always admired him and thought he was one of our smartest players. Dick was a big help with rookies and guards. Sometimes he was a little impatient when guys didn't learn things as quickly as he had. I can still hear the sound of his voice teasing some of the slow learners.

The ownership and management of the team also changed. Gulf and Western took over controlling interest. Ned Irish retired, and Mike Burke became president of the Knicks. Irving Mitchell Felt left and was replaced by Alan Cohen. I always had a good relationship with Felt, who had shared our glory years and two championships. He had a real feel for the sport of basketball and all the problems that could be associated with it. Alan Cohen was very different. Cohen was more of a corporate man, a bottom-line type of guy. Our rapport was not what I'd enjoyed with Irving Mitchell Felt.

Another big change we faced in 1974–75 was the lack of bulk and brawn on the team. We had John Gianelli, a good player, an excellent backup center, but not the force we needed. John was six foot ten, but had trouble keeping his weight over 200 pounds no matter how many malteds he drank. Late in the year we acquired Neal Walk, who had played in the NBA for six seasons before he joined us. Born in Brooklyn in 1948, Neal moved with his family to Miami when he was eight years old. He didn't like New York City too much. At six ten, with a thick dark beard, Neal sitting in a chair looked like a guy posing for Lincoln's statue in the Lincoln Memorial.

"I liked being back here in New York City for two days," he told me when he joined the team. "That's all I can take. Personally I enjoy being outdoors, seeing blue skies and tall mountains. But I can dig it if I can make a buck."

"If you get back to your old form, Neal, you'll make big bucks," I told him.

"Red, I'm not Willis Reed."

"I know, Neal."

"I'm not another Dave DeBusschere."

"I know, Neal."

"I'm my own man. I'm Neal Walk."

"That's clear to everyone, Neal."

"That's cool, Red." He smiled. Neal ended most of his sentences with "That's cool."

Divorced a short time before we acquired him, Walk weighed barely 210 pounds. He had once been a hulking 250-pounder. His diet now consisted of vegetables, fruits, beans, rice, soup, and nuts. He was Jewish, but he wasn't kosher, and he did a lot of drinking out of a jug that was labeled Purified Mineral Water.

We thought that Neal Walk might come back to his old form when he joined the Knicks, but he never did. The competitive juices had all been used up. Neal's mind was on other things, like alternate lifestyles. He was a disappointment. We became a team with a guard-oriented offense. Earl and Clyde accounted for about 41 percent of the club's scoring, what there was of it. We ranked 14th out of 18 teams in offensive average and somewhere in the middle defensively.

We were in Chicago on a promotional night, and the San Diego Chicken was doing his routine, running up and down, teasing fans and players. The Chicken had a habit of crawling into a team's huddle, then running to the home team's bench as if he had picked up some classified information.

During a time-out, our team was huddling and the Chicken came crawling in. He popped his beak in under my legs. I can't repeat what I said, but I'm sure the Chicken still remembers it.

"Coach, coach." That Chicken was startled. "Why are you getting so excited? This is just part of my act."

I was more than excited. I was furious at what I thought was an invasion of privacy and a burlesque of the game.

"If you don't get the hell out of here, you won't have an act—you'll be nothing but chicken feathers!"

The "Chicken" ran away. Not only cameras and mikes and chickens, but intrusions of any kind were barred from my huddles. Anything that hampered my concentration and that of the team was not welcome.

Around that time there was some controversy about women reporters being welcomed into the locker rooms. Some coaches and players were opposed to the women, but I welcomed them. I knew they had a job to do and I wasn't going to hamper them. Besides, I was always a supporter of the First Amendment. (I think that means I was in favor of freedom of the press.)

Some of the scenes in the locker room were kind of funny, though. Jane Gross of *The New York Times* was one of the first women sportswriters to come into our locker room. She entered, pad and pencil in hand, set to do some work. Suddenly Jim Barnett came up behind her and kissed her on the back of the neck. She jumped.

"Just being friendly," Barnett said. "I'm welcoming you."

"Would you do that to a guy?" I said to Barnett. I think he got the message.

An image that still remains in my mind is an interview Jane Gross did with Neal Walk. He had a towel around his shoulders—that's all he had on. Neal stood up and Jane stood in front of him. She didn't look up. She kept her head buried in her notebook and went about her business asking questions. I give women like Jane Gross credit—they had to have guts to be in with some of those guys.

We finished that 1974–75 season in third place in the Atlantic Division, 20 games behind the first-place Boston Celtics. Our record was 40–42, the first time in my Knick coaching career that one of my teams finished under .500.

Houston was our competition in the playoffs and they had the home court edge. They beat us in the first game on their court; we defeated them in the next game at Madison Square Garden. And we lost to them in the rubber match in Houston, and that was our season.

One of the bright spots of that year was Harthorne Wingo, who had the best year of his career playing in all 82 games, averaging more than seven points a game. He spent a lot of time getting taped by Danny Whelan in the dressing room. Danny had told Wingo that when he was the trainer for the Pittsburgh Pirates, Roberto Clemente had always liked to get taped a lot. I guess Wingo thought if it worked for Clemente, it was a good idea for him.

That season Wingo, a joyous player and a crowd pleaser, became a cult figure at the Garden. Fans would call out, "Wingo, Wingo!" urging me to put him in the game. Wingo sat at the end of the bench next to Henry Bibby, and whenever I'd glance down in Wingo's direction he'd get a little nervous. "Oh, no, Red. Oh, no," he'd say with a big smile on his face.

I always wanted all my players to be involved, especially the guys at the end of the bench. That's why it was nice to see the fans get behind a guy like Harthorne Wingo, but I was never influenced by what the crowd screamed. I ran the team. Yet, Wingo was an underdog—that's why the fans loved him and why I was fond of the guy.

Maybe all that screaming had an influence on Wingo because when the season ended he went a little Hollywood on me during the contract negotiations for the next season.

"I'm happy with the offer of fifty thousand dollars, Coach," he said. "But I think I'm worth fifty-one."

"Wingo." I was a little puzzled. "What difference is another thousand dollars going to make in your life?"

"You want the truth, coach? Or a bullshit story?"

"Give it to me straight, Wingo, I can take it."

"Well, Henry Bibby signed for fifty thousand, and I know I'm a thousand dollars better."

Wingo really wasn't a thousand dollars better, but he was hard-working and likable, so I gave him the extra grand.

Butch Beard, another likable guy, joined us as the Knicks got set for the 1975–76 season. A six-five guard who had been an All-American at the University of Louisville, Butch came to our club after playing with Atlanta, Cleveland, and Seattle.

He made an impression on me in our very first practice by picking up our offensive and defensive system immediately. No one I had coached before had ever done that.

"What are you, some kind of genius?" I asked him during the practice.

"Far from it, Red." He smiled. "It's just that I've been traded so many times that whenever the scouting reports came in I attempted to memorize every team's plays. It's memory, not genius."

The practice ended, and I gave all the guys a little break and told them to return in 20 minutes to watch a film. They all met the time deadline except Butch Beard, who showed up five minutes late.

"That'll be five dollars." I smiled at him and held up my old Bullseye watch. "You're five minutes late, Butch."

"I was trying to locate my contact lenses, coach. Nobody gave me the rules. I told Clyde I was going to be a bit late. Give me a break," Butch protested.

"Five dollars *is* a break, Butch, because it could be a lot more. Pay Danny Whelan later. Now let's all watch the movie."

Butch Beard was never late again, but others were, and they paid the price.

We got off to a lousy 8–19 start that 1975–76 season. Seven of our losses were by three points or less as our tempo broke down, and bad breaks haunted us. In a game against Seattle I set up a play for Bill Bradley from his favorite spot—the top of the key. His shot hit the back of the rim and went down almost to the bottom of the net and jumped out. We lost the game.

On October 23, 1975, we acquired Spencer Haywood and gave up a big bundle of cash. Spencer was 26 years old then, a great individual scorer at six foot eight and 225 pounds. I knew we needed to get some more offense or the season would be a total loss, so we went for him.

There was too much pressure placed on Haywood. The press called him the new Dave DeBusschere, and that wasn't accurate or fair. Unlike Dave's game, Spencer's style was dependent on individual stuff. Haywood had only 81 assists in 71 games—he just couldn't or wouldn't give up the ball. Haywood also had quite a few defensive lapses. It just wasn't good chemistry putting him together with Monroe, Frazier, Jackson, and Bradley.

In December 1975 I came back with the team to New York City after a long road trip to the West Coast. It was nice to be back home. "Mike Burke's office called," Selma told me. "He wants to see you as soon as possible and they left a message for you to call." I phoned the Garden.

"Mr. Holzman, Mr. Burke wants you to come in by Long Island Rail Road tomorrow on the 11:22 A.M. train," the voice on the other end of the phone told me. The voice sounded almost like a recorded message.

I usually drove in but the weather was kind of threatening so it was no problem taking the railroad. I spent some time in the smoking car, did justice to a good cigar, and made a lot of headway with *The New York Times* crossword puzzle. The train pulled into Penn Station. I got out and was headed toward Madison Square Garden when a beautiful young woman dressed in a trench coat came up to me.

"Mr. Holzman, Mr. Burke sent me. Would you come with me please?"

"Where are we going?"

"I'm sorry, Mr. Holzman, but I'm not at liberty to divulge that. It's only a short walk."

She didn't move as quickly as Walt Frazier, but she set a pretty swift pace. We had just crossed Seventh Avenue and were walking down Thirty-sixth Street when I practically bumped into Seymour Becker. Seymour and his wife, Stella, rented the cabana next to mine at the Sands Beach Club in Atlantic Beach, Long Island. I hadn't seen him since Labor Day.

"How are you doing, Red?" Seymour looked me and the woman over.

"Great, Seymour, I see you still got your tan from the club."

"Mr. Holzman," the woman cut in. "We really don't have much time. We must get going."

"Okay, okay," I told her. I shook Seymour's hand. "Sorry," I said. "Business before pleasure. I gotta go." We left a gaping Seymour, and I knew I would have to get to Selma before Seymour did.

We did a lot of roadwork before we finally arrived at our destination—the Algonquin Hotel. "How come we didn't take a cab?" I asked the woman. "It wasn't such a short walk."

"Mr. Burke didn't want us taking a taxi, Mr. Holzman. He felt we would be too conspicuous pulling up in front of the hotel that way."

She led the way into the Oak Room, a place where I knew all the literary and theater types gathered. Burke, spiffy as usual, nursed a drink at a corner table.

"Hey, Mike," I greeted him. "What's the idea of meeting here? There are lots of places closer to the Garden."

"This place is filled with celebrities, Red. No one will notice us here."

I looked around. Burke was right. At the next table was Anne Baxter. A few tables away was a guy who looked like Neil Simon. "I see what you mean, Mike," I said. That morning had begun to feel like a Humphrey Bogart movie.

The reason for the meeting was the suggestion from Mike Burke that I give up my role as general manager after the season and concentrate exclusively on coaching. When the team was winning, and things were stable, that hadn't been a problem. However, times had changed, and Burke's suggestion was not a bad idea. With all the recent turnover on the Knicks, I had been working like a horse as both coach and G.M. I agreed to give up the general manager job. Burke was pleased.

"Eddie Donovan is the man we have in mind, Red," Mike said. "It will be a way of reuniting a successful team."

"I have no problem with that, Mike," I told Burke. When we finished up our meal and finally parted company, I thought it was pretty strange to go through all that intrigue for such a simple meeting.

But then I remembered that Burke had served in the OSS during World War II. All that espionage and undercover stuff was probably still in his blood.

When I arrived home that night Selma greeted me with "Seymour Becker called."

"No kidding, Sel!" It had been a hell of a day.

It was also a hell of a season.

My throat was hoarse most of the time from all the yelling I had to do to get the guys on the Knicks to play as a team. I consumed a lot of cough drops and did a lot of gargling too. Selma's chicken soup came in very handy.

We were a weak rebounding team. We were a weak road team, winning just 14 of 41 games played away from the Garden. Our offense was nothing to write home about. Although Earl Monroe averaged 20 points a game and Spencer Haywood and Walt Frazier (who was injured and missed 23 games that year) both averaged 19 points a game, there was a big dropoff in scoring after that.

Despite the problems, we had some good moments as a team, and for a while it looked like we had a chance of making the playoffs. However, we hit a bad stretch near the end of the season, losing 22 out of 33 games.

The year turned out to be a disappointment. We wound up with a 38–44 record in fourth place. And for the first time, a Knick team coached by me did not make the playoffs.

BOOK THREE

CHAPTER 1

As the 1976–77 season began, I was described by the media as the dean of NBA coaches. I don't know if I was a dean, but I was certainly the oldest. At age 56, I was beginning my tenth season as Knick coach. I guess the funniest thing of all was that I never expected to be around ten years. When I took over in 1967, I thought I was just going to finish out the season until they could find somebody else. It didn't work out that way, though. It turned out to be a pretty good run for me. Other teams had changed coaches three, four times, but I was still doing my thing with the Knicks.

Change, however, was always part of the scene in the league, and that season was no different. The American Basketball Association had folded, and four teams from that league joined the NBA: the New Jersey Nets, Indiana Pacers, San Antonio Spurs, and Denver Nuggets. Some exciting players entered the league, including Julius Erving, who had been the ABA scoring champ three of the last four years. "Dr. J.", the main man for the Nets, was a dazzling player. Denver had good talent in Dan Issel, David Thompson, and Marvin Webster.

Some people in the NBA looked upon the ABA as a bunch of upstarts, and criticized the league for its wide open style of play. The former ABA teams were treated like new kids on the block. However,

I knew they were tough and talented kids. I knew that underestimating that talent could lead to some of our established teams getting hurt. A lot of them were.

Overall, though, taking in those ABA teams gave the NBA a shot in the arm. After a while the NBA even adopted the three-point shot that the ABA had used, which added some more excitement to the game. I'm glad, though, that the ABA red, white, and blue basketball was never adopted by the NBA. I always felt that it was a tough ball to play with. Those colors spinning around were distracting.

Things were spinning around on the Knicks as the season began, and we did all kinds of shuffling and scuffling to patch together a team. Bodies came and went. Neal Walk, Harthorne Wingo, Mel Davis, Eugene Short, and Jim Barnett all departed. In December, hoping to shore up our offense, we obtained Bob McAdoo, who had led the league three straight seasons in scoring; we also acquired Tom McMillen from Buffalo for John Gianelli and a lot of cash. We signed Dean "The Dream" Meminger as a free agent, but his best days were behind him.

The season got off to a lousy start—we lost three games in a row—and that set the tone for what was to come. We lost eight games by blowing big leads. Attention spans lapsed. Guys were going through the motions. Some of the players didn't believe in themselves.

In the early part of that season we finished a late game in San Antonio and had to catch a six A.M. bus the next morning. That meant a five A.M. wakeup. I was in the bus in my customary seat right next to the front door. Guys stumbled in, half asleep, carrying their stuff, moaning about the early hour. I counted heads and saw that Lonnie Shelton and Moe Layton were not accounted for. I stood up and made a big deal about looking at my watch.

"You know, Red," Butch Beard said, playing peacemaker, "your old ticker could be five minutes slow or ten minutes fast."

"That old ticker, Butch, is the official time for the team."

I looked at the watch. It showed six A.M. "By my time, it's time to go. Bus driver, close the doors!"

"Coach, I see two people coming," the driver said.

"Are they running?"

"No, sir."

"Then they're not with us. Close the doors and take off."

We took off and arrived at the airport and had to hang around waiting to board our flight. A cab came speeding up with Moe Layton and Lonnie Shelton in it.

"By my clock," I yelled at them, "you guys are late. That means that you're not out only the cost of the cab ride, you're both out 100 bucks each because you didn't catch the bus."

"Oh, coach, if I could only steal that grandfather clock," Shelton cried. I knew he and Layton were furious about being fined. However, they got over it, and paid up.

My little fines had always been part of my coaching repertoire, used to impress on players their responsibility to the team, to meeting deadlines, to doing what was expected of them. Unfortunately, that was the beginning of a time when players became more concerned with themselves than with the team. They thought more of the money they were going to make than the sacrifices they had to go through to play as a team. And that attitude showed on the court. Team stuff that I drilled into them broke down into individual stuff, and when plays broke down some new guys didn't have the intelligence or desire or discipline to go on with the options. They resorted to one-on-one play, since that's how some of them had been schooled. Today there's a lot of that in the NBA out of necessity, and sometimes the results are good. However, I always thought it best to run a play as a team for an easy shot.

There were quite a few team meetings. The old guard—Bill Bradley, Phil Jackson, Walt Frazier, and Earl Monroe—tried to reach the newer players. But the veterans were frustrated by what the new guys couldn't or wouldn't do—and the newer players were frustrated, too.

I did a lot of screaming, had a lot of one-on-one talks with players, cut playing time, tried different lineup combinations. At times I used a shuttle system in the backcourt. Butch Beard and Dean Meminger came in for defense; Walt Frazier and Earl Monroe were shuttled in for offense. The strategy behind those moves was to capitalize on the strengths and attitudes of players. Although Walt Frazier had always started at guard, I removed him for a time from that role after we went through a bad stretch, losing ten of 13 games.

"How can you do that to an institution?" a reporter asked.

"The only institution is the team," was my answer. However, I couldn't get the new guys to play a true team style. They were conditioned to playing their own way, doing their own thing. It was a very tough time.

Lonnie Shelton was one of the bright spots for us that 1976–77 season. Out of Oregon State, Lonnie was our most promising rookie in quite a while. For a six-foot-eight, 245-pound guy, Lonnie had the fastest hands of anybody on our team. He had a bit of a problem with the refs, who were not accustomed to seeing a bulky guy like him with such fast hands. They called 363 fouls on Lonnie, causing him to foul out of ten games.

It was a season in which I yelled a lot at Clyde the way I had picked on Willis in the past.

"Why do you take all that abuse from Holzman?" Walt was asked by a new writer on the beat.

"Red yells at me because he knows I can take it," was Frazier's response. "Red knows he's coaching the talent he has here now. He lets you play more one-on-one, lets us take our shots. In the past he didn't let us do things like that as much. The game has changed and he's changed with it."

Walt Frazier had changed a great deal, too, since I had first scouted him at Southern Illinois University. He had developed into an urbane and team-oriented player. When Willis had retired, I had appointed Walt the team captain.

Bill Bradley became a little more outspoken, seeing so many opportunities to win games pissed away.

"This team cannot perform under pressure," he told a reporter.

"What would you do if you were Red?" the reporter asked.

"I'd coach them in French."

When I started playing pro basketball I told myself I was going to do the best I could for as long as I could and hopefully not let anything bother my health. I knew one day somebody would tap me on the shoulder and tell me it's time to go.

There were twenty games remaining in the 1976–77 season, and we had no chance of making the playoffs. I knew it was coming, but I couldn't quit. I wouldn't quit. It was not in my nature to quit, but I knew a change was coming. Alan Cohen made the decision, and Mike Burke was the one who brought the news.

This time Mike and I met in my office in Madison Square Garden. The whole meeting lasted a little less than a half hour. The conversation was like a scene from a play with actors just reading the prepared lines. I sat in a leather chair behind my desk. Burke was seated on a chair in front of me.

"We appreciate all you have done for the organization," Burke began. "However, we think it's in the best interests of the organization that we make a change in coaches for next season."

I listened to him saying the words, doling out the clichés, his lips hardly moving. He was a pro, under control. It was all very low-key and friendly. Mike was doing his job.

"You know, Mike," I told him. "I could make a big stink and ask you how, after all I've done for the Knicks, you can do this to me. But I'm a realist. The team is in transition and having problems. A change is probably best for everybody."

Burke seemed relieved that I was going quietly. "Of course, Red, we are planning to pay you for the remaining year on your contract. You'll also become a consultant. We know all your knowledge will be invaluable to the organization."

"I guess that means not valuable."

"Red, you always could kid no matter the situation."

"Yeah." I lit up a cigar. "That was always one of my strong points."

"Everything will be worked out to everyone's satisfaction, Red."

"I'm glad, Mike."

"And we also want you to help us select a new coach."

That was it. Short and sweet. I was even going to have a hand in choosing my successor. I recommended Willis Reed. There was a press conference later that day set up to look like I was retiring. However, nobody was fooled; everyone knew that I had been fired.

It would have been nice to have gone out winning, but this was the time management had chosen, and I accepted it. I had been in pro basketball a long, long time and had done it all.

Our final game of the season was in Detroit, on Easter Sunday. It marked the end of a frustrating seven months: Eighty-two games and 24 road trips and a merry-go-round of hotels and motels, coffee shops and diners, jet plane rides from one end of the country to the other.

Before the game a guy came into the locker room. "Back on December 14, 1943," he began, "I was in the stands in Norfolk when you played on the Navy team against the University of Richmond, Red. And I've followed your career ever since." The guy handed me the program from that game.

"You saved this all those years?" I asked.

"Maybe you'd like it as a memento?"

"No thanks," I told him. "I have plenty of memories already."

With 1:48 left in the game, I looked down the bench and caught Phil Jackson's eye. "Go in there, Phil, and finish it up together with Bill Bradley."

With 1:35 left in the game, Bill hit a jumper from the left baseline. It was the last shot of his career. Ten years earlier, in a game against the Detroit Pistons at the Garden, Bill had played in his first NBA game. And he had hit his first shot, a jumper from the left baseline.

We won that final game against Detroit on Easter Sunday 144–126, but we didn't make the playoffs for the second straight year. And now another Knick team and another Knick coach would soon be doing what I had done for so long.

Through all those years of coaching and playing I never missed a game. Even when I had a virus, dental work, strep throat, I always managed to be there. When I coached in St. Louis, one year we trained in Mexico City. I came up with the *turista* disease. I was dying. If someone had taken a gun and shot me, they would have been doing me a favor. Thanks to team physician Dr. Stan London, I made it to the game.

That memory and all the others—grind and glory—were with me as I stepped down as Knick coach.

Despite my disappointment with that last year, I was still able to get a lot of pleasure out of Bill Bradley, Earl Monroe, Walt Frazier, and Phil Jackson. I loved how those guys tried to play the game the way it was supposed to be played—unselfishly. As we loaded up at the airport

in Detroit and got set for the trip back to New York City, I could tell
that the old guard on the team was kind of down.

"We did the best job we possibly could," I told them. There wasn't
much else to say.

Walt, Bill, and I had begun together on the Knicks a decade before.
We left together too. Bill retired. Walt would be traded. And I was
getting ready to function as a consultant.

I was 57 years old, kind of young for retirement; yet I honestly
never thought I would coach again. Nobody offered me anything, and I
probably wouldn't have taken a coaching job if it were offered outside
of New York City.

My time was spent taking it easy, going out to dinner with friends,
helping Selma with the shopping. It was nice not having to go to
training camps for those two-a-day practices. I went to basketball
games and watched the guy with the ball the way a fan does. There was
no pressure, no fights with refs, no jet lag from tearing around the
country. I developed an interest in tennis and played a lot of doubles.
My buddy Manny Feinberg and I took on all challengers: guys,
women, kids. We did very well on our own court. The only real
problems took place when we played against a pair of 80-year-old
ladies. They didn't respect the home court edge, and they cheated a lot.

My daughter Gail, who lived in Atlantic Beach, Long Island, had
introduced us to two women who belonged to our tennis club. They
were pretty good players and became our constant competition. We
must have played those women two dozen times when a daughter of
one of them came around after a game.

"Ma," the girl said as her mother walked off the court, "do you
know who you've been playing tennis with all this time? That's Red
Holzman—he used to coach the Knicks."

"Oh, come on," the mother said. "That's not Red Holzman.
That's Gail's father."

Looking back at that time, "Gail's father" was one of my aliases.
Another one that I got away with was "Knick consultant."

Willis Reed became coach of the Knicks, and I became a
consultant, but I was never consulted. They sort of pushed me
downstairs to a little office in an unused portion of Madison Square
Garden. All I needed was a place to sit, but the media made a big deal
out of the whole thing. One writer called the office "Holzman's exile to

Elba." Others claimed it was a sign that I didn't get along with Willis, and that he was keeping me out of the way.

As far as I was concerned, Willis Reed and I always got along. I had a lot of respect for him as a player. In fact, at the tail end of Willis's playing career, Alan Cohen was eager to place Willis on the expansion list and have him picked up by some new team. Management wanted to avoid paying Willis's big salary. I fought with Alan Cohen and convinced him that you don't place a guy like Willis Reed on an expansion list after all he had accomplished for the team.

Alan Cohen might have been right from a business point of view, but basketball is not just a business. It's a game, and Willis was a great New York Knickerbocker legend.

The Knicks finished last in the NBA in defense in 1977–78 but third in offense. Willis did a good job with the personnel he had. The team made the playoffs and defeated Cleveland in the first round. Philadelphia knocked them out of the playoffs in the Eastern Conference semifinals.

There were some changes in Knick management following that season. Sonny Werblin became president and chief operating officer of Madison Square Garden Center, in charge of everything that went on there. As the 1978–79 season got under way, there were many rumblings in the press about Willis and Sonny having problems with each other. Willis also was having some trouble with the media. I wasn't on the scene, so all the information I got was what I read in the papers.

"How can a player respect a coach he thinks may not be there the next day?" Willis was quoted in the newspapers. "Sonny Werblin has never given me a vote of confidence."

There were more rumblings after that. The Knicks got off to a 6–8 start. Then Sonny Werblin made his move. In a meeting that reminded me of the one I had when I was hired by Ned Irish to replace Dick McGuire, I was called in to meet with Werblin. The only difference was that I knew Irish well. I didn't know Sonny and had never made any overtures to him.

After the introductions, just like Ned Irish, Sonny got down to business quickly.

"Red, what do you think of Willis Reed's coaching?" he asked.

"All in all, I think Willis is doing a good job."

"We think," Sonny said, "it's in the best interests of the team that we replace him. Willis has created a schism with his statements in the press. He's made things out to be a 'we' and 'they' thing between him and the organization. He's lost control of the team. That's the reason for this meeting. Red, we want to bring you back as coach."

"But Sonny," I tried to joke my way out of it. "I'm enjoying retirement. I'm the women's tennis champion of my club. I'm having fun."

"Come on, Red," Sonny smiled. "You're not really having any fun. I'm sixty-nine and you're fifty-nine years old. I've been through retirement. I know that you work hard at trying to enjoy yourself."

"There are other guys around who would be perfect as coach, Sonny."

"You're the one we want." Sonny couldn't be distracted. "You have the qualities we want. You play within yourself. You're confident. You're a consummate professional with a perfect temperament. That's why we want you back."

There was a lot of hemming and hawing on my part, but being the good company man, I agreed to come back. We agreed that I would coach the Knicks for just two years, and then become general manager.

That year and a half that I was out of coaching hardly anyone came around to my little office. Now guys were busting the chops of security personnel to get directions. That little office never had so many people crowded into it.

I began my second stint as Knick coach under difficult circumstances. When I had replaced Dick McGuire as Knick coach, I took over a team that I had made. I had scouted most of the players, and had recommended drafting them. I knew them all very well, and they all knew me. When I replaced Willis, I took over a team I didn't make. In a way, they were a bunch of strangers.

I reinstated Frankie Blauschild as road secretary and business manager, appointed Butch Beard as assistant coach, and arranged for Fuzzy Levane to have a scouting job with the organization. As far as the players went, I knew they had mixed feelings about the change in coaches. I think most of them liked Willis, except the ones that didn't play. Most of the players didn't know me except by my reputation, and I knew I was an older guy in their eyes.

The roster had been shaken up quite a bit in the year and a half I was away. Earl Monroe had not signed for the 1978–79 season because of some problems with his contract. One of the first things I did was to convince management to bring Earl back.

Walt Frazier had been traded to Cleveland. I didn't know why the deal was made, but I always felt that Clyde should have finished up in New York City. Willis had been allowed to finish up his career with the Knicks. Clyde deserved the same treatment. If I had been coaching, I would have insisted that he receive it.

Lonnie Shelton was with Seattle where he had gone as compensation for Marvin Webster. Shelton was missed. He helped the Sonics win the NBA championship that year. I always thought Lonnie would be a great player and always liked him. However, management felt that acquiring Webster was more important.

That 1978–79 team had Ray Williams beginning his second year, Micheal "Sugar" Ray Richardson playing his rookie year, Marvin Webster, Bob McAdoo, Spencer Haywood, Glenn Gondrezick, Mike Glenn, Toby Knight, and Jim Cleamons.

The first game I coached was on November 11, 1978, at the Garden against the Boston Celtics. I stayed behind the curtain that led onto the floor until just a few minutes before game time. When I walked out a roar went up, and it got louder and louder. That ovation, by 18,906 fans—the largest crowd at the Garden to that point in the season—touched me. That was the most noise ever generated for me by any crowd except for the one at the seventh game at the Garden in 1970, when I walked out before we played L.A. for the championship. Of course, Willis Reed had just happened to walk out with me that time.

I sat on the bench and listened to the introductions of the players. And I thought about Eddie Stanky, who had returned to manage the Texas Rangers in 1977. After one game he decided to bag it and went home to his family. For me, it was just a passing thought.

We beat the Celtics 111–98. Our players worked hard, and I worked even harder—screaming out more instructions in that game than in any other one I could remember. Our guys needed direction.

"Get back."

"See the ball. See the ball."

"Slow it down, Ray."

"Use the clock."

"Don't stand, move, Marvin."

"See the ball. See the ball."

"Have an idea."

"Defense."

Bob McAdoo scored 36 points, Toby Knight had 19, and Ray Williams had 16 points and six assists. It was our defense, however, that did it as we held the Celtics under 100 points, the first time that season that a Knick team had held the opposition under the century mark in scoring.

Some of the guys were hyper in the dressing room after the game. "Practice tomorrow, twelve to two. Monday, ten to twelve," I told them. "There are going to be very few days off, if any. There's a lot of work to be done."

We won six of the first seven games I coached and in just one of those games did the opposition score more than 100 points. The media was enchanted by the crowds that had come back to the Garden, the tough defense that was being played, what seemed to be the new attitude by players they had called "overpaid underachievers."

I felt good about that fine start, and I knew we had some individual talent. But I also knew there was a long way to go before we had a team. The guys I was now coaching were a new breed, self-centered, and sometimes just plain selfish.

There were cliques on the team, and the younger and the older players were in constant contention with each other. Younger players like Ray Williams, "Sugar" Richardson, Toby Knight, and Gondo were in one group. Bob McAdoo leaned toward them, while Mike Glenn was on the borderline. The younger group wanted to take over but they really didn't have the maturity or steadiness to handle it.

Richardson and Williams were not thoughtful players, but they had so much talent that they were able to excel at times, to get by on raw ability. Other times, however, they looked foolish because they lacked discipline and didn't think out their moves. Some people compared Richardson and Williams to Earl and Clyde, two of the greatest players of all time. Although athletically Richardson and Williams might even be better than Monroe and Frazier, there's no comparison in basketball ability. Sugar and Ray were never in Frazier and Monroe's class.

Some of the players were curious about the championship teams I had coached, but I realized it was a mistake to dwell on the past.

"You guys have talent too," I told them. "The other guys have the reputation for what they accomplished. What we're concerned about is what we can do in the future."

Mike Glenn asked: "Red, how does it feel to be known as a household name?"

"It's not bad." I laughed. "It all depends on the household."

One of the things the team had done when Willis coached them was to have a shootaround the day of a game. Quite a few NBA teams followed that practice, which consisted of players spending about an hour shooting, walking through plays, and reviewing scouting reports on the team they were to play that night.

I had always been opposed to the shootaround in the past, thinking that it was best for players to rest on the day of a game. With today's players I realized the shootaround had some advantages as a refresher, plus the players were all brought up with it.

After I was on the job as the new coach for a few days Toby Knight popped the question that I knew was coming.

"Red, the other players are wondering—could we have a shoot-around as part of our routine?"

"Sure, sure, Toby," I told him. "If you guys think it has value and if we work hard at it, I don't see it doing any harm."

"That's great, Red." Toby was all smiles. "I'll tell the team."

They were all happy to get the shootaround, especially since it looked as if it was their idea. I knew that if the shootaround had seemed like my idea they would have been bitching about it for weeks.

Having a shootaround meant that guys would have to come into the Garden on the day of a game and then travel back to where they lived and then return at night for the game. It was a lot of wasted effort, so we decided to get them hotel rooms across from the Garden, where they could go and rest after the shootaround. It was a logical thing to do, but it was also a special privilege that we extended.

Unfortunately, some of them abused the privilege. Some of the players didn't use the rooms for the rest we had intended.

That wasn't the biggest problem. The biggest problem was lack of discipline. I was surprised that a team that had been coached by Willis Reed was so unruly. When he played for me, Willis was highly disciplined and brooked no bullshit.

I put in lots of hard work to create discipline on the team, to get them to play basketball my way. It wasn't easy. The only thing I could hold over them was denial of playing time. And that was a double-edged sword. It didn't make much sense cutting playing time from a guy who could win a few games for you.

One player, for example, was always the last one to show up for practice and the first guy to leave. He never gave the team an extra dime's worth of effort. An injury that many of the other players I coached would have shrugged off put him on the disabled list.

Naturally, every day we asked him if he was ready to play. "No, coach," he would mumble. "I'm not feeling well. I'm not ready yet."

This routine went on for a while. Then he showed up one night a half hour before a game.

"Coach." He was grinning. "I'm ready to play. Put me in."

I was pissed. "Hey, forget it," I told him. "Who the hell needs you now? You couldn't have told me this at one o'clock, at three o'clock so I could make the proper moves to get you off the injured list and put you back on the active roster? Why thirty minutes before game time?"

That was what he wanted to do.

We didn't have that much talent that I could do without him, so, being practical, I made the moves and was able to get him reinstated. He did help us win the game. But he wasn't going to be much help in the long haul.

Sugar Ray Richardson was picked by the Knicks, while I was away from coaching, in the 1978 draft. They could have selected Larry Bird as a junior, and he could have joined them the following year, but they wanted instant help. Boston picked Bird and waited, and he made them a great team. If the Knicks had had that kind of patience I could have coached Bird and might still be coaching the Knicks today.

Larry Bird would have made me a better coach and our players better too. He is a winner who leads by example, and our guys would have had to play the way he plays. Bird is cut in the mold of the players on my championship Knick teams, although he has more talent than any of those players. Those teams played the way Bird plays—

unselfishly or selfishly, whatever is needed. Larry hits the open man, plays hard all the time and can't tolerate other guys on his team not playing the same way.

So much for the fantasy. I didn't have Larry Bird to work with. I had Sugar Ray Richardson. And he was a big project. At times he'd play as if the basketball belonged only to him. In some games Sugar wasn't of any value to himself or to the team. I sat him down a couple of times during one game and tried to straighten him out. The first time he sat at the end of the bench and pouted. The second time he mouthed off.

"Shit, man!" Richardson screamed. "I can't play this way, coming in and coming out of a game. What the hell do you want?"

"I want some discipline. I want you into the flow. I want you thinking!"

"I play my game, Coach—and it's no worse than that of anybody else on this team and a lot better than most," he snapped. This was said in front of the whole team. I was furious! Not only had he shot his mouth off, but he also had publicly put down his teammates.

"Sugar"—we were face-to-face in front of the bench—"you sit for the rest of the game. If you keep your eyes and ears open, maybe you'll learn something."

Sullen, sulking, Richardson sat. He was a part of the team but apart from the team. There was a frown on his face, but I could tell he felt bad. He was a young, hyperactive kind of a guy, and I knew it bothered him to just sit and watch his teammates play while he was not able to.

When the game ended, Richardson came over to me in the locker room. "Red, I want to apologize to you for the scene I made," he said. "I wasn't thinking right."

"We all have times like that, Sugar. I accept your apology but I'm still going to fine you for your behavior. And you didn't just yell at me. You did it in front of the whole team, and you insulted them. I want you to apologize to the team."

"You're right, coach. I was dumb." Richardson's voice was almost cracking. I called the team together in the locker room.

"Sugar has something to say to all of you," I told them. "It's your time, Sugar."

He was a little sad-looking standing there in front of all of them.

"I'm sorry for the way I acted during the game," he said. "It won't happen again."

I knew it was hard for him to apologize, but I also knew Sugar was genuinely sorry. He got the apology behind him and was the better for it. I was never the type to bear grudges, and after that incident Sugar and I spent a lot of time together talking basketball, talking about what would be the best way for him to play. Sugar was a high-strung and sensitive guy, but he was able to see that I wanted him to succeed and that I was willing to go out of my way to help him.

In his rookie season Sugar played just 1,218 minutes, averaging just 6.5 points a game, shuttling back and forth between the forward and guard positions. He was erratic, always pouting, always moody about everything, going nowhere.

I spent more time with Sugar. "If you keep yourself under control," I told him, "and ignore all those guys who are instigating you, things will fall into place."

I switched him to point guard in training camp his second season and worked with him. He was a natural at the position, but he was also still a world-class brooder.

"Look at things this way," I told Sugar. "If you keep on doing well, you'll be making a lot of money, and a lot of fans for yourself. That will help you keep your sunny side up."

Sugar laughed a bit at that comment but followed my advice.

I began to call Sugar "Meshugeh." He liked that. He was from Denver, and he must have thought I was speaking French.

Sometimes in team meetings when I went over the roster I would emphasize the accomplishments of "Meshugeh" Ray Richardson. And Sugar would smile.

Then one day he came into my office and said he had to speak to me about a private matter. He sat down and in that high pitched voice he asked, "Why do you think I'm nuts?"

"I don't think you're nuts. In fact, I'm nuts about your ability. You have no limit to your potential."

"Okay, Red, then stop calling me Meshugeh. I found out what that means. It's 'nuts' in Yiddish."

I looked him in the eye. I was going to tell Sugar my George Mikan "schmuck" story. And then I thought of telling him how a negative word can be an endearing term. Instead, I just said, "Okay, Meshugeh, from now on just the short and sweet version for you, Sugar Ray."

"That's cool, man" was his response. He popped up and out of my office, another satisfied customer. At least for now.

Along with the other changes I instituted, I decided occasionally to discard my Brooks Brothers suits for more casual dress—jeans and shirts with epaulets which were in style then. There was no hidden motive, it was just more comfortable.

One writer arranged a meeting with me and killed an hour asking questions about what he called "Red's New Look."

"What do you think of jeans?" he asked.

"They're comfortable," I answered.

"Do you have a favorite brand?"

"No, do you?" I kidded him.

"I do, Mr. Holzman," he said, "but you're the interviewee, the respondent. And I am the one charged with the duty of ferreting out your views on the subject."

I could tell he was deadly serious. "Okay." I changed my look to that of a respondent. "Ferret away."

He ferreted.

I responded.

He ferreted some more and I responded some more.

A few days later, after all the ferreting and responding, the writer's article appeared in the newspaper. He had come to the conclusion that "Red's new look is a great help—really a wonderful thing—a tool that enables him to relate to the present day National Basketball Association athlete." *Relate* was a big word in those days.

Although the article was a lot of bullshit, at least the guy took a positive view. In my opinion, my clothes had nothing to do with how well I related. Relating, to me, through my entire coaching career, was always the same. You relate well if you treat people fairly. With some of those players on the Knicks at that time, relating meant bending over backward to give them the edge. I never did that. I always prided myself on treating everyone—substitute and superstar—the same.

Throughout the good times and the bad I also made it a practice not to let the game get to me, not to take it home with me. Some coaches ranted and raved, put on a big show of suffering. I felt that served no constructive purpose, and I never allowed the game to affect my health—win or lose, I always started fresh the next day.

"Don't defeats get to you?" a reporter asked me. "How can you remain so calm and cool even after a defeat?"

"I still sleep well at night and still eat the same meals and am still the same guy," I told him.

When that quote came out in the press, it was blown up a bit. Sonny Werblin read it and misunderstood it. He said he wanted a dedicated coach and after reading what I said, he wondered how dedicated I was. Maybe he understood only what he wanted to understand at the time.

We had a little meeting. "Sonny," I told him, "there are other things more important than basketball—like life and death. And there are guys who are dedicated one hundred percent and guys who are dedicated one thousand percent to the game. I fall into the one thousand percent category."

That little meeting cleared the air, and Sonny and I became better friends after that. I also developed a friendship with Jack Krumpe, back then a bright young executive assistant to Sonny, who later became the head of Madison Square Garden.

Sonny got a lot of newspaper space that season when he traded Bob McAdoo, our big scorer, to the Boston Celtics for three draft choices. John Y. Brown, who owned the Celtics, and Sonny got together one night in a restaurant and made the deal. They wrote it out on a napkin. As the coach, I didn't like that being done without my consultation. It was done, however, and the boss did it. And it didn't turn out to be too bad a deal. We were ultimately able to get two starters out of the deal— Bill Cartwright and Sly Williams.

We also swapped Spencer Haywood that season for Joe C. Meriweather. It was a good swap since we wanted to move Spencer, who wasn't playing that much and didn't blend with our team style. He had a bigger reputation, but Joe C. was a fine guy and a solid basketball player who could play center or forward.

Earl Monroe played in 64 games that 1978–79 season, averaging only 12 points a game, but he was a help to me with the younger players—a kind of link between what had been and what was. Even with the Pearl on the scene I knew I had my work cut out for me. We wound up the season with 38 wins and 44 losses in fourth place in the Atlantic Division. The only consolation for Knick fans was that the Boston Celtics finished behind us in fifth place.

CHAPTER 2

One of my best releases from some of the pressures of that time was a gourmet club named Lucullus, after a Roman general and epicure. I founded the club with my friend Al Aquilino, president of Lincoln-Ford on Eleventh Avenue in Manhattan. Mannie Brandt and I were the only Jewish guys in the group. Most of the members were Italian businessmen. We met on Mondays once a month at Alfredo's Restaurant on Fifty-ninth Street and Central Park South. Eating took place in the back room, and each of us took turns making up a menu. I learned then that not all Italians like garlic, because they always complained that I had too much of the stuff included in the dishes I made up.

I always liked a good meal in pleasant surroundings, and through the years I was amazed by the eating habits of players I coached. All of them had their own style and their own tastes.

The biggest eater of them all was Mel Davis. Mel was the kind of guy who could literally finish off an entire menu. He would order a chicken dinner and do that justice and then order a big steak. It was no problem for him to consume a double portion of pasta. Along the way he would clean out all the rolls and drink a still of water.

Bill Bradley had no time for food—he was always reading and couldn't wait to get back to his books. The kind of eater who would go to a coffee shop and order a steak and read a book, Bill also made a ritual of seeking out the nearest street vendor and sampling a hot dog and a soda.

Mike Riordan was a perfect example of a New York City working-class eater. Beer and fast food were his speed. Mike loved to go to Blarney Stone restaurants, stand up at the counter, read a newspaper, and have his hot dogs and chili. He was the kind of guy who couldn't seem to eat without a newspaper in front of his face.

Cazzie Russell craved service. One waiter or waitress would never be enough for him. Caz would usually need four or five, one for condiments, another for the water, another to talk to. If he saw a waiter unoccupied, Cazzie would occupy him by asking for another knife, spoon, or napkin.

Walt Frazier was really into nutritious foods, but he tried to keep it a secret. He'd eat fruit all day long, have a big salad for dinner, always watch out that he ate healthily. Walt took great pains with his diet—and it showed. He was always in great shape.

The classiest eater was Walt Bellamy. He liked always to eat in fine restaurants. And he knew how to eat—his table manners were very neat, and he knew his way around a menu.

The worst eater I ever saw was Dick Barnett, who might eat breakfast, but that would be all he would eat all day long. Dick was always in great shape, but I don't know what kept him that way. He could sit down to eat with the best steak in front of him and take two or three bites out of that steak and be finished. He slept a lot—maybe that's what made up for his poor eating habits.

John Gianelli was a pretty good eater, but no matter what he ate it disappeared on him. We really did try to fatten him up with malteds, but it didn't work. He didn't gain any weight at all.

Eating with good company was one way I got away from it all. Another release from pressure was fooling around, taking some shots at the basket after team practices. Marvin Webster heard about my shooting and one day challenged me to a ten-shot contest from the top of the key.

We each threw ten dollars on the floor. Marvin shot first. He made nine out of ten shots and bent down to pick up the ten dollars.

"Wait a minute, Marvin. I didn't go yet."

"An old guy like you probably can't even reach the basket. The money is mine, Red."

"It's no one's, Marvin, until I take my shots."

I took my shots. Not only did I reach the basket, I made nine out of ten shots. I could have made them all, but I didn't want to ruin Marvin's confidence. Besides, it was probably enough of a shock for him to see a guy using an old-fashioned two-hand set shot.

That shootout reminded me of an encounter I had with Dolph Schayes when I scouted for the Knicks. Schayes and his Syracuse team were finishing up their practice. I was there all dressed up in my Brooks Brothers suit while Dolph had broken a good sweat.

"Hey, Dolph, I'll shoot you five shots for fun and we'll see who's better. I won't even take my suit jacket off."

"You gotta be kidding, Red. You're not in shape."

"Well, let's give it a try anyway, Dolph."

Schayes, a guy with great pride in his shooting ability, took up the challenge. He made four out of five. I made five out of five. Dolph wasn't too happy, and insisted on a rematch.

"As long as we both live," I told him, "I'll never give you a rematch. You're one of the greatest shooters ever and having beaten you is something I want."

Schayes started bitching and moaning and chased me all over the gym, but I wouldn't give him a rematch. Whenever we meet today, we kid about that time. Dolph still wants the rematch, but he'll never get it.

Our number one pick in the 1979 draft was seven-foot-one, 240-pound Bill Cartwright out of the University of San Francisco. We were lucky to get him. The Knicks hadn't had a big guy with such fine tools and such a great attitude for quite a while.

For the 1979–80 season I hired Hal Fisher to team with Butch Beard as assistant coaches. In basketball for most all his life, Hal had coached United States Army teams and helped coach our Olympic teams. He's an outstanding teacher and I realized a lot of that teaching needed to be done for the players on the Knicks.

One of my most memorable wins took place at the Garden on November 20, 1979, in a game against the Houston Rockets. We were just terrible in the first three quarters, fumbling away the ball, missing easy shots, looking like we were sleepwalking.

We were down by 23 points with 13 minutes left in the game, down by 18 with just eight minutes left. Some of the fans in the small crowd of 8,953 were on their way out when Bill Cartwright missed a shot and then followed up with a stuff of his rebound. With 1:44 remaining in the game we trailed 117–110, and still more people left the Garden. Two free throws by Ray Williams cut the Houston lead to five points.

I replaced rookie Hollis Copeland with rookie Geoff Huston. "Take a three-pointer, Geoff, make a three-pointer."

Huston followed orders and made me look like a genius. He hit a three-point shot and we trailed 117–115 with 39 seconds to go.

Even though Moses Malone had scored 32 points and pulled down 14 rebounds for the Rockets, killing us all through the game, I took a calculated risk and told our guys to foul him.

At the line with three chances to make two points, Moses missed his first attempt. Then he missed his second attempt. The die-hard Knick fans, the regulars, were in an uproar. They waved jackets, arms, and programs. Moses shot for the third time. The ball hit the right side of the rim. Richardson rebounded. Toby Knight had the ball, but he was tied up and passed to Larry Demic who shot and missed. Hollis Copeland rebounded and twisted back up and hit the lay-up. The score was 117–117 as regulation time ran out.

We rolled all over the Rockets in the OT, holding them to just one field goal, and won the game 130–125.

"These are the glory days," I told the press after the game was over. "The glory days are now."

It was a tremendous win, my 500th as an NBA coach. It was a comeback victory to stack alongside our scoring five points in 15 seconds to keep alive the 18-game winning streak in 1969–70. It was a victory that gave me the same kind of charge.

Maybe I got a little carried away, along with everyone else, by that come-from-behind win. Glory days turned into a glory day. Most of that season with the 1979–80 club was one long struggle to gain an identity. That Knick roster had five rookies, one sophomore, and three guys playing in just their third year in the NBA.

We lost quite a few games that we should have won. Calls went against us in favor of more veteran teams. I adjusted my coaching to the circumstances and to the personnel. Offense became our strong suit with Bill Cartwright at the hub of it.

Someone once came up with the idea that I don't use rookies that much, but actually it depended on the quality of the rookie. Bill Cartwright was a rookie who worked hard and always adapted to what was required of him. Bill was smart enough to know that it was important for him to play team basketball, to share the ball and the burden in a game. He realized that the guards and the forwards had to be compatible with the center. In that system Bill got the ball and scored his points. He wound up having a great year, playing in all our 82 games, averaging almost 40 minutes and 22 points a game.

Cartwright, Ray Williams, and Toby Knight combined for almost 60 points a game. Micheal Ray Richardson blossomed at point guard and led the league in steals and assists. We posted the fourth best team scoring average in the NBA.

However, our last game of the year kind of symbolized the season for us. With just seconds remaining in a game against Philadelphia, Micheal Ray Richardson threw an inbounds pass right into the hands of Julius Erving. The "Doctor" went the length of the court, put both knees into Toby Knight's chest, and dunked the ball. That basket won it for them at the buzzer. Nobody called the foul, and the loss was a downer. We could have wound up the season at 40–42 if we had won, and we would have been in the playoffs. We had to wait 24 hours to see if the Nets would beat Washington to enable us to squeeze into the playoffs. Unfortunately, that didn't happen.

Going into the 1980–81 season, we acquired Campy Russell, a good addition. He passed well for a 6–7 forward, had a good knowledge of the game, and was team-oriented. In training camp I worked the players very hard, and finally settled on the 12 guys I was going to use. The media made a big deal about the fact that the 12 players I selected were black. It was no big deal to me. In my mind those players were the best talent available. But there's no question that this was a far cry from the days at Rochester when Fuzzy Levane and I ate meals in a hotel room with Dolly King because he didn't want to be embarrassed in restaurants.

All the players on that 1980–81 team knew their roles. The starters knew they were going to get a lot of playing time, and the others knew what was going to be expected of them. We had a good system. Guys knew who, when, where, why they were going to play.

Bill Cartwright was backed up at center by Marvin Webster, and

Marvin understood that was his role. At times I played both Cartwright and Webster at the same time. They were both over seven feet tall and the press called them the "twin towers."

Micheal Ray Richardson and Ray Williams were the starting guards. Sugar had a lot of respect for Ray and both guys got along well together. Mike Glenn's job was to come in and replace either Sugar or Ray. I always liked having the flexibility of three guards.

Sly Williams and Campy Russell were fine passing forwards, and at times I interchanged them with the guards and at each forward position. Sly was one of the best instinctive players I ever saw, excellent at getting inside position off the boards.

In the training camp for the 1980–81 season I spent a lot of time with Sly, just as I had with Sugar the year before. In 1979–80 Sly had played in just 57 games and hadn't scored much. He wasn't that happy with his situation. I explained to Sly what his role would be and showed him how to adjust his moves on the court to be more effective. That picked up his game.

We were able to get some good minutes of play out of Mike Woodson, our top draft choice that season, and Larry Demic, our second draft pick from the year before. DeWayne Scales and Reggie Carter were the guys at the end of the bench, but they helped when they were called on.

It was a young team, and an inexperienced team, but it was a team with a lot of potential. I had some frustrations with them trying to get them to execute set plays properly. We would have a set play working, but it was not quite at the tempo that was required. The 24-second clock would run down on them quite often, and to compensate for that we had to resort to one-on-one at times.

Despite all this, the team was getting into a pattern of play that I liked. A good feeling was being established among the players. It was a situation similar to the one I had with the championship Knick teams in that players knew what was expected of them, and the whole of the team was becoming more important than its parts. They were learning my style.

I even had them playing some good team defense. We held other teams to nine fewer points a game that season than we had the year before when we were third from the bottom of the league in defense. We also wound up with a 22–19 road record compared to a 14–27 mark the season before. And that was one of the key things in our successful season.

Another big factor was the ability of those players to come back and win games that they were losing. We must have come from behind in 20 games that looked like sure losses. The good chemistry on the team, the cooperation between the players on the court—these things kept us in games to the end.

Individual stats were good too. Richardson was fourth in assists and second in steals in the league. Ray Williams was fifth in steals, and he wound up with Bill Cartwright among the top 20 scorers. Sly Williams and Campy averaged 28 points between them; altogether we had five guys who averaged in double figures in scoring.

A milestone in my coaching career took place near the end of that season, on Saturday night, March 2, 1981, my one thousandth game as a Knick coach. They dimmed the lights at the Garden before the game with the Chicago Bulls. Then there was a brief ceremony, and Ray Williams made a little speech. I was given gifts, including a video recorder. It was a nice gesture. I still have the thing, but I never figured out how to use it. Selma, who they called "the real coach," was given a bouquet of roses.

We lost the game to the Chicago Bulls as the guys missed six of their last eight free throws. I would have given away everything I received that night if only we could have won. The media built up the game as a "Holzman milestone," pointing out that my Knick coaching record was 571 wins and 429 losses and that my NBA total of games coached—1,203—was second only to Red Auerbach's 1,417.

After the game was over I sat in my office, relaxed for a while, puffed on a cigar, and listened to the questions posed by the press.

"Are milestones important for you, Red?" a reporter asked.

"Oh, yeah." I took a puff on my cigar.

I could tell that wasn't the answer he wanted.

"Don't you have any other thoughts about the one thousandth game you coached?"

"Not really," I told the guy. I wasn't putting him on. "It just means that I've been around for a long time and that I have been a survivor."

Inside of me there were other thoughts, but I didn't feel like sharing them. Besides, had I told those thoughts to the reporters, they probably would have thought I was being corny. I wondered where all the years had gone, what the years ahead had in store. I thought about how unbelievable it was that I had been in the league through the 1940s, the 1950s, the 1960s, the 1970s, and now at sixty years of age I was still doing my thing in the 1980s. I thought about how the jet had replaced the old cars we used to ride around in to get from one basketball game to another. And I thought about how one-on-one play and slam dunks and three-point shots had opened up the game. I thought of how much I loved basketball, the way I always felt inside about the excitement of the game, the crowd, the thinking ahead about what moves to make—and when they worked out, what a kick that was!

We finished the regular 1980–81 season with 50 wins, the seventh best record in the league. And we made the playoffs, the first time a Knick team had made the playoffs since 1977–78. I felt great and so did the players. Since I had taken over the team from Willis Reed, we had moved from 31 wins to 39 wins to 50 wins.

The Chicago Bulls were our competition in the best two of three games of the Eastern Conference playoff qualifying round. We had won seven more games than the Bulls during the season and were favored over them. Toward the end of the season we had beaten Chicago badly on their home court. I sent Butch Beard to scout the Bulls during the last week of the season.

"Chicago is a much better team," Butch told me, "a much improved club than when we played them. Artis Gilmore [their center] was flat when we saw the Bulls. His game is up, Red. He's become more mentally aggressive and picked up the whole Chicago team."

I passed on the information Butch gave me to our players. A bit concerned about overconfidence on the part of our guys, I was also worried that they were going into the playoffs with minimal experience against a more mature club.

There were also a lot of quotes in the newspapers attributing statements to our players putting down the Chicago team. It came out that they were happy to play Chicago, who they said they could beat easily. Those quotes stirred up the Bulls, and I'm convinced it made them play harder. I always believed it was best not to try to win games in the newspapers because you might win them there and lose them on the basketball court.

Chicago beat us in the opening game at the Garden, holding us to just 80 points as Ray Williams and Micheal Ray Richardson just wouldn't give up the ball. Unfortunately, they weren't the only players who didn't perform as they should. Most of the team played out of control.

Before the second game I tried to steady the team down. During a long meeting I explained that the defeat was just one game in a two-of-three series.

"We can beat the Bulls," I told the guys, "if you think out there, if you help each other out."

That second game was a hell of an experience that placed tremendous pressure on our kids playing in just their first few years in the NBA. The Chicago fans put the home court edge on parade, making so much noise that we couldn't even hear ourselves in the huddle. We had to resort to writing instructions down on a pad so our players could understand what we wanted them to do.

Despite the crowd noise and the inexperience of our players, we pushed the Bulls into overtime. Unfortunately, we lost, 115–114. If we had managed to get past that game, who knows what might have happened. However, we didn't get past that game, and what had been a winning and satisfying season for the Knicks ended too soon, and on a sour note.

That disappointing playoff experience created some panic. A lot of people in the media overreacted. Management and I overreacted too. We should have taken our lumps, relaxed for a while, gone back the next year, and learned from our playoff experience. We should have stood pat or just tried to add a player or two.

Part of the problem was that players were beginning to get very conscious about becoming free agents and renegotiating contracts. There was a great deal of turmoil over money. Management back then was very concerned about not running up any red ink. They didn't want to pay Ray Williams what he was asking, and he wound up with the Nets. Today management's biggest problem seems to be figuring out ways to spend more money.

I was never one to say: "Buy me this player. Buy me that one." However, we should have paid Ray Williams what he was asking and kept the team intact. Ray was important not so much for his own ability but for the way I was able to use him and work him in as a part of the whole that was the team.

We made some deals to add some more experienced players. Maurice Lucas came over from the Nets as compensation for Ray Williams. A big strong guy with talent, Lucas had a lot of trouble playing any kind of pressing defense. He was demanding about needing and getting an inside position under the basket, always wanting to exploit the post down low. It was difficult to break Maurice of the habit. Cartwright's game suffered. Lucas kept taking up the space Bill needed to wheel in and go to the basket.

Mike Woodson was traded for Mike Newlin who had been the leading scorer for the Nets the year before. That was another mistake. Woodson was a good kid, a class guy who fit in very well with my team concept.

Newlin never fit in. He was a guy near the end of his career and his attitude showed it. He lacked intensity except when it came to spending time taking what he told people were Bible lessons over the telephone.

The homework that should have been done on the Woodson-Newlin trade was not done by our organization. I didn't really have the time to do the homework myself. I had enough on my hands just coaching the team and trying to get it respectable.

Mike Glenn was shipped off to Atlanta for a number two draft choice. Trading Glenn, our number three guard and a perfect spot player, was another mistake. The rap on Mike was that he was slow and not aggressive, but he too was a very important part of the whole. Mike was a great shooter, an intelligent guy. Everyone on the team liked him and that meant they would give him the ball when he got open and also run some plays for him. Sometimes a guy is a great shooter but he doesn't get the ball. If Mike had screens set for him he could put the ball in the basket. They called Glenn the "Stinger" because he could sting teams with his shooting within a team concept.

We wanted to shore up our guard situation, so we acquired Randy Smith from Cleveland for a number one draft pick. Smith was a nice fellow, but he was not for us. We wound up having to find playing time for four or five guards and Randy was unhappy. He moaned that he didn't get enough minutes. At that time Randy had going for him the record for playing in the most consecutive games and was very anxious about keeping it. I wanted to help him and made sure I played him in every game so that he could keep the record going. Still he bitched about not getting enough playing time.

There were just too many guys who needed playing time. We had Cartwright, Webster, Lucas, Russell, Sly Williams, Larry Demic, Alex Bradley, Toby Knight, Reggie Carter—too many big people. We had Sugar Ray Richardson, Mike Newlin, Randy Smith, Hollis Copeland, and Paul Westphal near the end of the season—too many guards. I was in a situation similar to that of the New York Yankees a few years ago, when they had two or three players for certain positions. The guys who didn't play were unhappy; the ones who did were worrying about the time when they weren't going to be playing.

Beyond that, the guys who left were replaced by guys who didn't fit in. That's not to say that the new guys weren't good players in their own right, but their chemistry, their way of playing, was not for us.

Some players also didn't get along with each other. There was bickering and bitching, jealousies and ego problems. And some guys just didn't like other guys—it was as simple as that.

Micheal Ray Richardson was constantly getting himself and everybody else crazy. He was disruptive, always hassling to get his contract changed. We had to live with it since Sugar was one of our important players.

Everybody on that team was also always thinking of money. They had one eye on the basketball and the other on what the other guys were getting paid. It was bedlam—one of the most frustrating periods in my entire coaching career.

The system I had developed the season before was totally disrupted. I always thought a team was better off with seven or eight guys who knew their roles. It's really tough to give 11 or 12 guys decent playing time.

When a guy writes a book he can put in it whatever he wants. I've read enough books to know that—and I've been around basketball long enough to know where all the bodies are buried. I could say right in this space that the deals, the trades, the panic that broke up the good system I developed were someone else's doing, that I had no part in it. However, that's not the way it was. I did have a hand in it, along with Sonny Werblin, who was in charge of the entire Knick operation, general manager Eddie Donovan, the scouts, and the assistant coaches. All of us contributed to the decisions that were made.

The thing that amazed me was that all through my years with the Knicks, decisions were always announced in the press as a "we" thing. If things went well or if things went badly—it was always "we" who were involved. Then everyone shared the responsibility in the press for the decisions that were made. During those last months I looked around, and "we" were no longer making the decisions. There was only "me." And that was not the way it was. It was a bit disappointing for me to take most of the heat for that last year. I didn't like what had happened, but I lived with it. I didn't whine about it then—and I'm not going to whine about it now. I never did like a whiner.

On Sunday, April 18, 1982, I coached my final game for the New York Knicks. We lost 119–99 to Boston. The Celtics finished in first place with a 63–19 record, while we were fifth in the division with a 33–49 record.

"Red Holzman is a great coach," Boston's coach Bill Fitch told reporters. I guess Bill was paying me back for some of the nice things I had always said about him. "If Red were sitting on my bench with my players and I was sitting on his bench with his type of players, he would have a record that matched ours."

I was 61 years old when the 1981–82 season ended. Before I turned 60 I used to have a recurring dream; I was very unhappy with myself. I was still playing basketball, but I couldn't make a lay-up or pass the ball properly. I would tell myself that things weren't that bad because although I was playing poorly, how many guys my age could still be playing at all? When I turned 60, the dream stopped.

My coaching stopped after the 1981–82 season. Sonny Werblin made me a consultant for the remainder of my contract. I realize now that if you stay too long they judge you on what you did at the end. And if the end was no good they judge you on that. The way it ended was a downer for me, the players, management, and Knick fans. You're never happy to be finished under those circumstances. Looking back now, I realize it would have been better for me to have gotten out after the 50-win season of 1980–81. I would have gone out on top with a team I developed.

BOOK FOUR

I still make the drive in by car to Madison Square Garden that I made hundreds of times when I was Knick coach. I go through the Queens Midtown Tunnel, down Thirty-fourth Street and pull up at the Garden and honk my horn. The corrugated gate comes up. The guards still know me.

"Hey, Coach," a guy shouts. "How you doing tonight?"

"Fine," I say. "How are you, pal?"

I like the fact that I'm still remembered, that I'm still thought of as a part of the Knick family. Only sometimes I get the feeling that one day I'll drive up and honk my horn, and the gate won't come up.

I still pull for the Knicks when I watch the road games on TV or attend most of the games at the Garden. Sometimes when I am in Madison Square Garden my eyes look up into the rafters, and I catch a glimpse of the NBA championship flags from 1969–70 and 1972–73. It's a nice feeling for me to see them hanging there.

We won two championships. The Celtics and the Lakers have won many more. However, I think the two titles that we won really started something in the NBA. We played almost perfect basketball, unselfish basketball. It did a lot for the league at a time when the NBA needed something like that—a great team in New York City.

Playing in New York City has certain benefits, as well as certain problems. The media is very demanding, as are the fans, and they should be. However, once you show them that you're giving them what they want, or at least making the effort to give them what they want, then they're the greatest fans in the world.

We were so visible doing things that hadn't been done before that television picked us up, national magazines focused on us. We attracted a kind of cult following. At the time we were never satisfied that we played well enough, but as the years have passed I now realize that our kind of team played a unique and pleasing kind of basketball.

Before the Knicks, most championship teams were built around one dominant player—George Mikan, Bill Russell, Wilt Chamberlain. Our team was built around six or eight guys playing as a unit, able to execute almost perfectly. There was very little one-on-one stuff. We spent a lot of time freeing up a guy for an easy shot. Individually they had their minds on who was going to be free and where the next pass was going. Today there's a lot of time spent freeing up a guy so he can go one-on-one. That's one of the major differences between my teams and today's style.

In 1986 the NBA drew more than twelve million fans—an all-time record. That was a far cry from the early days and even my time. The coaches keep getting better and better. The NBA today has a very intelligent, very able group of coaches.

Two of my former coaches—Nat Holman and Lester Harrison— plus my old teammates Bobby Davies and Bobby Wanzer are enshrined at Springfield. Several players that I coached are also in the Hall of Fame: Willis Reed, Bill Bradley, Walt Frazier, Jerry Lucas, Dave DeBusschere, Bob Pettit, Ed Macauley, Slater Martin, and Cliff Hagan. It's a good feeling to know they have been recognized and that I in some way contributed to their being there.

I was at the Hall of Fame induction ceremonies in 1985. My old teammate Al Cervi was admitted, along with Nate Thurmond, who played some great ball against our Knick teams. Women were admitted to the Hall for the first time. Three women went in as coaches and contributors. As time goes by I am sure there will be more women admitted—people like Nancy Lieberman, Anne Myers, Carol Blasjowski.

On May 6, 1986, I was enshrined in the Basketball Hall of Fame. I never get very emotional, but I did get pretty excited over my acceptance into Springfield. And it was unusual for me because it was a singular honor. I've always worked for team basketball. That's been my thing. And although they singled me out as an individual, the Hall of Fame induction was still a team thing. I know that if it had not been for the guys who coached me and those I played with—when I was very young, and later in high school, college, the pros—I would never have gotten into the Hall of Fame. I never dreamed when I was starting out that I would achieve that goal. It was not until I had coached for a while that I thought a bit about the Hall of Fame. Of course I always *hoped* I would be inducted, but I never thought it would happen to me . . .

The guys inducted alongside me were Billy Cunningham and Tom Heinsohn as players, coaches Stan Watts from Brigham Young, Fred Taylor from Ohio State, and Red Mahalik, a referee. I had had contact with all of them through my career: Cunningham and Heinsohn had played against my teams; I had scouted teams coached by Taylor and Watts; and Mahalik was the ref in some of the games I coached.

I made the drive from Cedarhurst to Springfield with Selma, Fuzzy Levane, and his wife, Kay. It was a beautiful spring day, and we had a lot to talk about. The trip there was like coming full circle in a way—Fuzzy and I driving in a car, talking about the old days—it reminded me of trips I used to make when I was coaching or when Fuzzy and I often drove up to training camps together. It also reminded me of the times Fuzzy, Les, some other guys on the Rochester Royals, and I would travel by car from city to city, game to game.

There were more than a thousand people at the Hall of Fame festivities. For me it had the feel of an old movie. I was looking around for Red Sarachek, Irv Siegel, Matt Pressman, Eddie Loik—guys like them and others from the Workmen's Circle and high school days who helped me progress to become a good basketball player. None of those guys were there, but there were others: Lester Harrison, Bob Davies, Al Cervi, Bobby Wanzer, all guys from my old Rochester team.

Each of the Hall of Fame inductees was escorted to the microphone and presented with a plaque and a ring. Les Harrison presented me with mine. My speech was light and brief. Later I thought I should have said a little more—some of the other speeches were emotional and much longer. But talking a lot has never been one of my strong points.

I'll say one thing for that day in Springfield, though. During my career in basketball I received seven rings: one for being on an NBA championship team in Rochester; two for coaching the Knicks to championships; two for coaching NBA All Star teams; one for coaching in the NBA Legends Game, and my seventh was for induction into the Basketball Hall of Fame. And although all six rings I previously received have a lot of significance, the seventh ring, the Hall of Fame ring, I realized that day, was the most important to me. It's the crown jewel of my basketball life. The first six rings I received were really what enabled me to get it, but now I know why people say seven is a lucky number.

One of the things that gives me a lot of satisfaction is seeing so many of the players I coached and people I competed with and against still going strong.

Bill Bradley is now a United States Senator from New Jersey. Danny Whelan and I still look forward to Bill becoming president of the United States and collecting those chits Bill owes us. Although Dave DeBusschere is no longer involved in basketball, he has served as head of basketball at Madison Square Garden, Commissioner of the ABA, and general manager of the Nets. I'm sure he'll find another slot in the league soon.

Walt Frazier works out of New York City, is involved with the United States Basketball League and represents players. Earl Monroe is the commissioner of the new United States Basketball League, functions as an agent, and keeps busy with his recording company.

Phil Jackson has been coaching in the Continental League, basketball's top minor league, and also following in my footsteps coaching in the Puerto Rican Summer League. Phil has his sights set on an NBA coaching job.

Jerry Lucas works with religious groups, teaching them how to memorize the Bible.

Poor Nate Bowman died of a heart attack in 1985.

Willis Reed moved from his job as an assistant coach with the Atlanta Hawks to become an assistant coach with the Sacramento Kings.

Mike Riordan has a very successful restaurant that he and his wife run in the Washington, D.C. area. Butch Beard was with the Knicks and did a very good job as a color commentator for their games. Walt Bellamy was the Tiler in the Georgia legislature under Jimmy Carter.

Howie Komives had a few Wendy's hamburger restaurants, but he sold them and did very well. Cazzie Russell has coached in the Continental League and the USBL.

Frankie Blauschild and Eddie Donovan just recently left the Knicks. Frankie was the business manager; Eddie was a vice president in charge of player personnel. And Dick McGuire still holds down my old chief scout job that he took over on December 28, 1967.

Dick Barnett still dresses in his old elegant style and for a time published a *GQ* type magazine. And Dean Meminger coached for a while in the Continental League and in women's basketball.

Les Harrison remains in Rochester where he promotes the Kodak Classic, a college basketball tournament each Christmas season. Les is still productive even though he's up in years. When he was admitted to the Basketball Hall of Fame—achieving what he said was his life's ambition—he was very happy that all the work he had done was rewarded.

Ben Kerner left basketball after selling his St. Louis Hawks some years back. For a time he owned a franchise in St. Louis in the indoor soccer league. Fuzzy Levane was working for the NBA supervisor of officials. He's retired now, and we get together quite often.

At various functions I run into George Mikan, who has a very successful travel agency business in Minneapolis. Bobby Wanzer, my old teammate on the Royals, was athletic director at St. Johns Fisher College in Rochester. Harry Gallatin is a dean at Southern Illinois University.

I don't know where Charlie Eckman is, but I read a quote in the newspapers attributed to him: "There are two plays in basketball. One is putting the ball in the basket and the other is South Pacific." That sounds like Charlie.

Nat Holman is retired and lives in Manhattan. He's getting on in years, but he still makes appearances at significant basketball games and events. And we get together and talk about the old days quite a few times a year.

Vince Boryla has done very well in business and is president of the Denver Nuggets. In 1985, he was voted NBA executive of the year. Johnny Green and Tom Hoover are still in the New York area. Green, the first of the players I scouted who made the Knicks, owns a McDonald's on Long Island.

During the Knick championship years I became pretty good friends with Dustin Hoffman, who came to a lot of the games and sat behind our bench. We've kept up our friendship. In 1984, Dustin suggested I try out for the role of Charlie in *Death of a Salesman,* a play he went on to star in that had a very successful Broadway run.

At the rehearsals I waited for my chance to read. I thought Chuck Connors probably began that way, and Jim Brown and Joe Namath, too. Then I chickened out. The actors that were reading were so convincing and had so much talent that I realized I couldn't compete.

"Dustin," I said. "I'm really a movie actor, not a stage actor. I've got to be in a situation where, if I make a mistake, I can do it over. Think of me for the movie role."

Acting is really not my thing. Mine has been a basketball life, a long basketball life. When I finished up I had won more games than any other coach in NBA history except for Red Auerbach. Other coaches have passed me on the all-time winning list and there will be more as time goes by, but I take some pride in my accomplishment.

I also found out from my stockbroker Bob Wallach's son Adam, who is a statistical whiz, some interesting stuff about myself. I'm the only person in NBA history to have coached in four decades and the only one who was a player, coach, and general manager in five decades. Being around a long time does create some interesting stats.

I am always running into guys from the past in all kinds of places, and it's funny how many of them are from my old neighborhood in Brooklyn. The scenes are always pretty much the same.

"Hiya, Red," a guy comes up to me. "How are you doin'?"

I always say "Fine! And how are you?"

We stare at each other for a couple of moments and then the guy usually says: "Don't you know who I am?"

"I'm sorry. I really don't remember," I tell him. "Give me a hint. Help me out."

"I'm Handsome, Handsome from the old neighborhood. We used to be good friends." Funny thing is, the guys from the old neighborhood never give me their real names; they always use the names they were known by, their nicknames . . . Lippy, Wimpy, Jay Bird, Fred Boy, Big E, Handsome.

"How long ago was that?" I ask.

"Oh, about forty-five years ago."

I look at the guy who calls himself Handsome. He's about five five, he's a little on the heavy side, he's bald. No way in the world would I ever recognize him.

Those encounters with guys from the old neighborhood really show the passage of time. And I know that they could never recognize me after all this time except for the fact that I was in basketball, in the public eye—in newspapers and on television—for all those years.

So for all of you guys who are still around whose feelings might've been hurt when I didn't recognize you—I want all of you to know I didn't mean anything wrong. I still have a soft spot for all of you.

At Knick games, or when I'm in a restaurant or at the theater, people I never knew come up to me. Although they represent a cross-section of society—cab drivers, business executives, teachers—they all seem to be part of a team, and all say about the same thing.

"Red, I just want to shake your hand and thank you for the many years of enjoyment and great basketball you gave me."

It's nice that they come over, that they feel comfortable enough to come over. Those meetings always make me feel good, and until they started happening I never realized how many people enjoyed what we were doing.

In Yiddish, there's a word, *nakhes*. It means obtaining pleasure and enjoyment from the achievement of others. I experienced a lot of *nakhes* myself from basketball, because all I really ever earned in my life came from the game. That's why this book is dedicated to the fans—the fans in New York City who won a lot of games for us by not quitting and not letting us quit, the fans in Rochester, the fans all over the league. Fans have thanked me in a lot of places, and this book is my way of thanking them. They gave me *nakhes*, too.

WILLIAM (Red) HOLZMAN

Born August 10, 1920 in Brooklyn, N. Y. Height 5:10. Weight 175.
High School—Brooklyn, N. Y., Franklin Lane.
Colleges—University of Baltimore, Baltimore, Md.,
and City College of New York, New York, N. Y.
Signed by Rochester NBL, 1945.

Acquired by Milwaukee NBA from Rochester NBA, 1953.

—COLLEGIATE PLAYING RECORD—
Baltimore

Year	G.	Min.	FGA	FGM	Pct.	FTA	FTM	Pct.	Reb.	Pts.	Avg.
38–39					Statistics Unavailable						

CCNY

Year	G.	Min.	FGA	FGM	Pct.	FTA	FTM	Pct.	Reb.	Pts.	Avg.
39–40					Did Not Play—Transfer Student						
40–41	21	...	...	96	...	...	37	...	...	229	10.9
41–42	18	...	...	87	...	...	51	...	...	225	12.5
Varsity Totals	39	...	...	183	...	...	88	...	...	454	11.6

NOTE: In Military Service during 1942–43, 1943–44 and 1944–45 seasons. Played at Norfolk, Va., Naval Training Station and scored 305 points in 1942–43 and 258 points in 1943–44.

NBL AND NBA REGULAR SEASON RECORD

Sea.—Team	G.	Min.	FGA	FGM	Pct.	FTA	FTM	Pct.	Reb.	Ast.	PF	Disq.	Pts.	Avg.
45–46—Roch. NBL	34	...	...	144	...	115	77	.669	...	...	54	...	365	10.7
46–47—Roch. NBL	44	...	...	227	...	139	74	.532	...	...	68	...	528	12.0
47–48—Roch. NBL	60	...	...	246	...	182	117	.643	...	...	58	...	609	10.2
48–49—Rochester	60	...	691	225	.326	157	96	.611	...	149	93	...	546	9.1
49–50—Rochester	68	...	625	206	.330	210	144	.686	...	200	67	...	556	8.2
50–51—Rochester	68	...	561	183	.326	179	130	.726	152	147	94	0	496	7.3
51–52—Rochester	65	1065	372	104	.280	85	61	.718	106	115	95	1	269	4.1
52–53—Rochester	46	392	149	38	.255	38	27	.711	40	35	56	2	103	2.2
53–54—Milwaukee	51	649	224	74	.330	73	48	.658	46	75	73	1	196	3.8
Totals	496	...	...	1447	...	1178	774	.666	...	...	658	...	3668	7.4

NBL AND NBA PLAYOFF RECORD

Sea.—Team	G.	Min.	FGA	FGM	Pct.	FTA	FTM	Pct.	Reb.	Ast.	PF	Disq.	Pts.	Avg.
45–46—Roch. NBL	7	...	...	30	...	31	21	.677	...	...	10	...	81	11.6
46–47—Roch. NBL	11	...	...	42	...	29	22	.759	...	...	22	...	106	9.6
47–48—Roch. NBL	10	...	...	35	...	15	10	.667	...	...	6	...	80	8.0
48–49—Rochester	4	...	40	18	.450	6	5	.833	...	13	3	...	41	10.3
49–50—Rochester	2	...	9	3	.333	2	1	.500	...	0	3	...	7	3.5
50–51—Rochester	14	...	76	31	.408	34	23	.676	19	20	14	...	85	6.1
51–52—Rochester	6	65	15	3	.200	6	1	.167	6	2	3	0	7	1.2
52–53—Rochester	2	14	5	1	.200	4	1	.250	1	1	4	0	3	1.5
Totals	56	...	...	163	...	127	84	.661	...	...	65	...	410	7.3

NBA COACHING RECORD

Sea. Club	Regular Season W.	L.	Pct.	Pos.	Playoffs W.	L.	Sea. Club	Regular Season W.	L.	Pct.	Pos.	Playoffs W.	L.
1953–54—Milwaukee ...	10	16	.385	4†	..	..	1973–74—New York	49	33	.598	2§	5	7
1954–55—Milwaukee	26	46	.361	4†	..	..	1974–75—New York	40	42	.488	3§	1	2
1955–56—St. Louis	33	39	.458	2T†	4	4	1975–76—New York	38	44	.463	4§	..	..
1956–57—St. Louis	14	19	.424	1†	..	..	1976–77—New York	40	42	.488	3§	..	..
1967–68—New York	28	17	.622	3‡	2	4	1978–79—New York	25	43	.368	4§	..	..
1968–69—New York	54	28	.659	3‡	6	4	1979–80—New York	39	43	.476	3T§	..	..
1969–70—New York* ...	60	22	.732	1‡	12	7	1980–81—New York	50	32	.610	3§	0	2
1970–71—New York	52	30	.634	1§	7	5	1981–82—New York	33	49	.402	5§	..	..
1971–72—New York	48	34	.667	2§	9	7	Totals (18 Seasons)	696	604	.535		58	47
1972–73—New York* ...	57	25	.695	2§	12	5	*Won NBA championship.						

†Western Division. ‡Eastern Division. §Atlantic Division.
NBA Coach of the Year, 1970. . . . Coach of NBA championship teams, 1970 and 1973. . . . Ranks second among NBA's all-time winningest coaches. . . . Member of NBL championship team, 1946. . . . Member of NBA championship team, 1951. . . . Named to NBL All-Star First Team, 1946 and 1948. . . . NBL All-Star Second Team, 1947.

INDEX

A

Abdul-Jabbar, Kareem, 87, 99, 118, 119, 126, 134–36
Alcindor, Lew. *See* Abdul-Jabbar, Kareem
Alexander Hamilton High School, 10
Allen, Lucius, 134, 136
Allen, Woody, 92–93
American Basketball Association (ABA), 59, 157–58
American Hockey League, 23
Antony and Cleopatra cigars, 111
Aquilino, Al, 173
Atlanta Hawks, 91, 119, 190
   see also Milwaukee Hawks; St. Louis Hawks; Tri Cities Blackhawks
Auerbach, Red, 47–48, 53, 137, 179, 192
Azenberg, Manny, 74

B

Baltimore Browns, 38
Baltimore Bullets
   name change, 136
   playoff games, 85, 98–99, 119–20, 126–27, 143
   shutout, 89–90
Barker, Cliff, 24
Barnes, Jim "Bad News," 53, 54, 55
Barnett, Dick
   comments by, 73, 91, 102, 122, 138
   leisure time, 75, 84, 174, 191
   non-player roles, 129, 145
   scoring, 79, 99, 101, 110
   team position, 62, 64, 83, 87, 95, 104, 111, 120, 125, 134, 141, 142
Barnett, Jim, 147, 156
Barry, Rick, 68–69, 76
Barth, Morris, 7
Basketball Association of America (BAA), 23, 24, 26
   see also National Basketball Association; National Basketball League